SUDDEN MIRACLES
Eight Women Poets

SUDDEN MIRACLES

Eight Women Poets

Edited by
RHEA TREGEBOV

SECOND STORY Press

CANADIAN CATALOGUING IN PUBLICATION DATA
Tregebov, Rhea
Sudden Miracles
ISBN 0-929005-26-0

1. Canadian poetry (English) — Women Authors
2. Canadian poetry — 20th century I. Tregebov, Rhea, 1953-.

PS8283.W6S84 1991   C811'.5408'09287   C91-094894-1
PR9195.3.S84 1991

Printed and bound in Canada

Second Story Press gratefully acknowledges
the assistance of the Ontario Arts Council and The Canada
Council

Published by
SECOND STORY PRESS
760 Bathurst St
Toronto, Ontario
M5S 2R6

CONTENTS

INTRODUCTION 11

ROO BORSON

Statement: A Few First Principles 35
Snowlight on the Northwood Path 38
Intermittent Rain 40
We're Out with the Night Beings 42
Poem Beginning with a Line by Anne Michaels 44
After a Death 45
The Thinker, Stone Orchard 46
Save Us From 47
Leaving the Island 49
Starting the Tape 50
It's Raining 52

SUSAN GLICKMAN

Statement: But Why Poetry? 57
Henry Moore's Sheep 61
Beauty 74
Silverprint 76
Kodachrome 78
Families 79
One 81

CLAIRE HARRIS

Statement: A Real Good Lemonade 87
Policeman Cleared in Jaywalking Case 90
Where the Sky is a Pitiful Tent 94
Black Sisyphus 103
Framed 105

ELISABETH HARVOR

Statement: Down Here, Down There 109
Down There 118
The Sky or the Forest or the Cupboard 120
In the Hospital Garden 122
Madam Abundance 126
At the Horse Pavilion 131
Saturday Afternoon at the Clinic 133
Bloom, Rain 137

PAULETTE JILES

Statement: You There 143
Going to Church 147
One Sister 151
Song to the Rising Sun 156

ANNE MICHAELS

Statement: Unseen Formations 173
Lake of Two Rivers 180
Miner's Pond 185
What the Light Teaches 193

ERIN MOURÉ

Statement: And Poetry/ 209
Jump Over the Gate 212
Fifteen Years 214
Thirteen Years 215
The Beauty of Furs 216
The Beauty of Furs: A Site Glossary 217
Tucker Drugs 218
Naming a Poem Called Tucker Drugs 220
Seebe 222
Nice Poetry 227

BRONWEN WALLACE

Statement: One More Woman Talking 237
Daily News 245
The Man with the Single Miracle 248
Familiars 253
Food 257
Anniversary 262
Koko 265

ACKNOWLEDGEMENTS

ROO BORSON "Snowlight on the Northwood Path," "Intermittent Rain," "We're Out with the Night Beings," "Poem Beginning with a Line by Anne Michaels," "After a Death," "The Thinker, Stone Orchard," "Save Us From" and "Leaving the Island" from *Intent, or the Weight of the World* by Roo Borson. Used by permission of the Canadian Publishers, McClelland & Stewart, Toronto. "Starting the Tape" and "It's Raining" used by permission of the author.

SUSAN GLICKMAN   All poems used by permission of the author. "Henry Moore's Sheep," "Beauty," "Silverprint," "Kodachrome," "Families" and "One" from *Henry Moore's Sheep and Other Poems*, Véhicule Press.

CLAIRE HARRIS   All poems used by permission of the author. "Black Sisyphus" and "Framed" from *Travelling to Find a Remedy*, Goose Lane Editions. "Where the Sky is a Pitiful Tent" and "Policeman Cleared in Jaywalking Case" from *Fables from the Women's Quarters*, Williams-Wallace.

ELISABETH HARVOR   All poems used by permission of the author. The author's statement "Down Here, Down There," is a slightly revised version of the article which is forthcoming in *Event*.

PAULETTE JILES   "Going to Church" from *Celestial Navigation* by Paulette Jiles. Used by permission of the Canadian Publishers, McClelland & Stewart, Toronto. "One Sister" and "Song to the Rising Sun" from *Song to the Rising Sun*, Polestar Press.

ANNE MICHAELS   "Lake of Two Rivers" from *The Weight of Oranges*, Coach House Press. Used by permission of the author. "Miner's Pond" and "What the Light Teaches" from *Miner's Pond* by Anne Michaels. Used

INTRODUCTION

It's always the chance word, unthinking
gesture that unlocks the face before you.
Reveals the intricate countries
deep within the eyes. The hidden
lives, like sudden miracles,
that breathe there.

— Bronwen Wallace,
"Common Magic"

THE WORK OF THE EIGHT REMARKABLE POETS represented in this collection does indeed unlock for readers the intricate countries, the sudden miracles of women's lives. Here our lives as women are no longer hidden. One of the most basic, and most controversial, challenges feminism has made has been the challenge to language: from the search for gender-free terms to the dream of a common language. Poetry has a special role to play in this struggle to enlarge our awareness of the power and the pitfalls of the language given us. When it is unquestioned, language may appear to be a neutral medium; the bland, blank vehicle through which we communicate our everyday needs. Poetry, by drawing attention to language *as* language — its look, its sounds, its grammatical ambiguities — works against the grain of these assumptions. By making us conscious of language, poetry makes language problematic; it disrupts the smooth, unbroken surface of linguistic convention.

The poets included in this collection are marked most, perhaps, by the variety of their strategies at taking hold of language and making it their own. They share, however, a commitment to the creation of new kinds of meaning, of breaking through the accepted norms to a meaning more consistent with their lives and with the lives of those around them. Whether or not they are writing about what we traditionally have considered "female subject matter," their writing proposes a new set of values, a more multi-valent and complex view of reality, of the lived core of our lives, than is offered by the dominant culture, the mass media, the best-sellers. In the very late twentieth century, this alternative vision is crucial. It is crucial to our development as a genuinely human society; crucial, I believe, to our very survival as a species.

I've chosen in this collection to present a focused view; to give readers the opportunity to encounter, *in depth*, eight extraordinary writers within the critical context of this introduction and the authors' own aesthetic statements. Given the current tremendous difficulties of distribution and promotion poets face, it seems a valuable method. This is a personal selection which no doubt demonstrates the strengths and fallibilities of such an approach. The book is not a new canon, nor is it a comprehensive, catholic survey representative of the breadth and range of poetry that Canadian women are producing. These are simply the writers whose work, over the last decade and more, I tracked in magazines; whose next book I anticipated eagerly; whose development I followed with a mixture of awe, envy, admiration and trepidation. It is an opportunity for readers to share the combination of good luck and good grace that brought these women's work into my life, a sequence of encounters fueled by my deep need, as writer and as reader, for models, colleagues, traveling companions, guides.

I cannot separate the works from the women and perhaps the best I can offer the reader here is a sense of living presence. I hope the format of this introduction, and of the book itself, assists readers to a degree in feeling that these writers are *incorporate* here. That they are living women (with the tragic exception of Bronwen Wallace) who breathe their lives into the work.

❖

Perhaps what I value most about ROO BORSON'S poetry is the rad-
ical way in which she repositions human beings within the natural
world, redefining the human. Borson sees us as inextricably linked
with nature, with both the inanimate and animate world. Her vision
is about as far as you can get from the hierarchical view of nature,
the notion of a Great Chain of Being which positions the patriar-
chal God at the top of the hierarchy and the inanimate world at
the bottom. (Women fall somewhere in between.) Borson instead
maintains a remarkable global perspective on things and on our
place in things. As "We're Out with the Night Beings" shows, the
apparently "other" world of nature is, precisely, our own world. Her
perspective is both detached and interested, dispassionate and keen.
The work asserts the connectedness between the human and the
natural without sentimentality and without falling into the "pathetic
fallacy" of anthropomorphism. Perhaps this is because she is so
scrupulous with language; she is a poet as much in love with lan-
guage as she is with the natural world, and it is a fruitful passion.

Such an orientation and such precision make the cat in "Starting
the Tape," the dog in "It's Raining," the rain itself in "Intermittent
Rain" — even those bentwood chairs in "Snowlight on the
Northwood Path" — play a role they could play in no one else's
work. They have a life; they carry a weight, an authority of being
that, while it may be instructive to our understanding of our lives,
is not ancillary to human life. It is perhaps because of this faith in
the livingness of the non-human world that Borson's descriptions
are so precise and vivid, so original. In these remarkably visual
poems, description is more than description — it is an embodi-
ment, an enactment of the real thing.

Borson's leveling gaze can initially bewilder her readers. We
are not accustomed to finding ourselves *among* things rather than

above them. We are not accustomed to so much life outside ourselves. Borson's identification with the natural world is so strong that her sense of self is, at moments, almost undistinguished from her surroundings. The boundaries between the observing self and the universe observed are remarkably transparent. This lends an impersonal, alien quality to the work, a quality both intriguing and strange. By denaturing the natural, the human, by making it strange, Borson makes it perceptible, enables us to see beyond the limitations of personality, beyond the limitations of our species-centred point of view.

This lack of intrusive personality, which Keats called the poet's negative capability, enables the observed subject to live and speak while the poet steps quietly into the background. But the perceived neutrality of Borson's voice is not straightforward. In many of the poems, this neutrality is deceptive, ironic, suspect; clearly at odds with the specificity and particularity of perception expressed. By, for example, appropriating the bodiless voice of scientific discourse, of presumably detached, objective observation which stands in clear contrast to the individuality of the observations being expressed, Borson creates a tension in the work which urges readers to their own conclusions, their own queries and arguments.

Borson continues to redefine the lyric, particularly within the elegies of her most recent work. She has always sung the individual as the convergence of countless natural forces — evolution, geography, memory. In the elegies "Poem Beginning with a Line by Anne Michaels," "After a Death" and "It's Raining," the loss of such convergence is lamented, and the continuance of the non-human world takes on a poignancy, an emotional resonance that was not as marked in earlier work. This is Borson at her richest, where the human is neither inflated nor diminished.

SUSAN GLICKMAN not only writes very well, she writes well about an increasingly ample and profound range of subject matter. Her thoughtful voice has contributed to Canadian poetry an intelligence imbued with articulate compassion. Few of us write with such a powerful combination of knowledge and feeling.

While Glickman's body of work has often taken the work of art as a point of departure for the examination of the human, her long poem "Henry Moore's Sheep" is perhaps her finest piece yet on this topic. It is also sure evidence of the liberating effect on the imagination of an integrated, mature feminist analysis. Glickman's observations have as much to contribute to our understanding of the social as they do to our understanding of art. With devastating wit and humour, Glickman takes on sculptor Henry Moore, one of the icons of male, western culture and gleefully lays bare the rather basic gender assumptions underlying his artistic production. The investigation makes very convincing art criticism; it also makes terrific poetry. Glickman's quick, ironic, assured intellect roves over the cultural artifacts in an unanxious, yet querying way.

The poem is a thoughtful, delightful meditation on the hows and whys of objectification. Glickman speculates that it was Moore's unremitting gift of observation that forced him to move from a portrayal of the sheep as mere glyphs, abstractions of the notion of inelegant physical presence, to one in which they are ineradicably particular, individualized. He does so, she notes, to the point that his sheep have more wit than his women.

Glickman manages in this argument to both gift us with the work of art and to critique it. The accuracy and precision of her imagery enables us to envision the drawings at the same time as it forms and colours our perception of them. As readers, we are allowed to share the development of her analysis as we are shepherded gently from insight to insight. Glickman's control over tone is impeccable, and the poem thereby has a rhetorical power that convincingly draws her readers into her point of view.

Glickman is equally formidable when she turns her attention to the dynamics of family; to, as she would put it, apprehending feeling in time. Looking backwards, at family history, she observes how family mythology forms our truest inheritance, how it shapes the lives of the generations that follow. In "Beauty," Glickman paints a vital portrait of the patriarchal, unyielding grandfather who nonetheless bequeaths a troubling, but forceful, model of authenticity of self.

In "Beauty" and in the paired poems "Silverprint" and "Kodachrome," the stubborn knot of family, of self as defined within family, is teased into meaning. Glickman manages to eloquently recreate the child's apprehension of things and at the same time to provide an adult, and mature, understanding of that apprehension. What maturity provides is perspective. While we all retain our childish, solipsistic sense of the mystery of our parents' or grandparents' lives before our birth, as adults we are haunted by our inability to grasp them as individuals separate from our own needs. What do these childish paradigms obscure? In "Silverprint" and "Kodachrome" Glickman captures our wonder at the gap between before and after, the mysterious leap from their shadowy lives before us to their life as us, as part of the constellation of our childhood. She evokes in these poems as well the loss this inevitable misapprehension entails, and evokes perhaps most forcefully the helplessness of human love.

The depth of Glickman's understanding of human love, and of the raw pain and power that the family contains, is perhaps most evident in "Families." This moving poem reveals the fragility of the family structure. Again looking back, Glickman provides a tough, affecting depiction of the family in conflict. Glickman is particularly astute and penetrating in her portrayal of the helplessness of fathers before their fatherly wishes, of their imprisonment in a masculine role that, in the end, obscures the self, keeps them out of focus. The falsity of the goal — the cardboard perfection of the cereal box family — does not diminish the pain of the failure to achieve it. The strictures of convention are not enough to keep the family from the chaotic waters of their real antagonisms. The poem, however, looks not only backwards towards the past, but forwards to the possibility of creating a new family, and to the belief that this movement is worth the risk. The honesty of this poem stuns, as does the courage of its movement towards a more hopeful future.

Glickman's emotional perspicacity leads often to hopefulness. Perhaps it is the generosity of her vision, her lack of solipsism, her ability to reach out to the breadth and depth of others' experience (whether it be the world of art or of the infant) that prevents her from an easy despair. The poem "One" is a particularly powerful example of this extension of the self, this imaginative remembrance. In this piece Glickman shows a remarkable sense of connection to the perceptions of a very young child. The poem comprehends the hereness and nowness of the child's world, while it laments the imminent loss of this ability to perceive fluidity, to avoid the stasis that an organized perception requires. Glickman's tolerance for remaining in the chaotic midst of things allows us as readers to inhabit the child's world, to participate in the "one flower in the world, all there is of yellow." Her access to that reserve of joy she wishes for the child, a joy which she has clearly maintained within her, becomes ours, and it is a rare gift.

CLAIRE HARRIS' poetry derives its strength from contradiction: the tension between the language of literature and the language of testimony; between the private and the public, the indigenous and the immigrant self; between the voice that privilege makes authoritative and the authentic voice. Her work speaks of the psychic and political ravages arising out of these contradictions with dignity, assurance and conviction. Harris' insistence on formal complexity as well as on the complexity of her subject matter, her inventive use of deconstructivist theory to disturb our notions of poetry, has a political as well as aesthetic intent. The challenge to the reader's assumptions occurs on the level of form as well as content. Harris interrogates the conventions of poetic form on all fronts: by manipulating and refashioning syntax; by transforming grammar to her own means; by including within the poem the prose statement, the newspaper item, the verbatim transcription.

The sequence of prose poems which make up "Policeman Cleared in Jaywalking Case" opens with an extract from an *Edmonton Journal* article. From it we learn that the African jaywalker in question, who was "arrested, strip-searched, and jailed in the adult detention centre," was a fifteen-year-old schoolgirl. Harris compares the incident to a similar one in her own childhood in Trinidad, an incident in which the sense of community overrode the need to impose authority. The poem confronts the purblind prejudice of Canadian society which sees a criminal in a terrified kid.

Harris addresses the apparent conundrum of simultaneously taking advantage of and subverting the power of the oppressor's language by a powerful synthesis. She combines traditional oratorical structures, the ABCs of rhetoric, with a fragmented, disjunct syntax. In this way Harris succeeds in expressing both the inadequacy of the language as we have it and the potency of her own visionary challenge. The schoolgirl's failure to produce identification for the policeman becomes, in the forceful logic of the poem, a symbolic and transgressive refusal to signify, to accept the false signification of the racist system which denies community to those it has defined as "other."

In this poem, the tolerance which ignores difference is inappropriate; to retain human meaning, the poem has a moral imperative to draw the line between the African self and the European society that denies that self. The eradication of identity, the loss of the soul is risked if the distinction between the self and those social structures which both seduce and oppress is allowed to become blurred. The poem refuses to participate in the semiotics of racism, to permit identification with that which is ultimately destructive.

In the affectionate, clear-eyed portrait of the father in "Black Sisyphus," Harris further develops this defiant emphasis on saying "no," on the refusal to be complicit, to participate in false signification. In this poem, the subversive speaking against the grain of the dominant discourse becomes a participation in a new creation, an Edenic naming.

In "Framed," Harris exposes the dangers of participating in false signification, in false identification. The protagonist in the poem has rejected her island heritage while fulfilling her mother's dreams of a better life which is the inverse of her own, a life in which the daughter is served, not servant. Harris reveals in the daughter a self so fractured that it cannot be grammatically expressed by a single pronoun: the alienated self, the self in exile, is referred to as "you," while "I" is used for the original, authentic self. What might appear at first glance pronoun chaos is in fact a brilliant grammatical device, a usurpation of the rules of grammar to express a different and dissenting vision.

"Where the Sky is a Pitiful Tent" juxtaposes Harris' own lyric fiction about a woman whose husband sides with Guatemalan rebels with the testimony of Rigoberta Menchú, a native Guatemalan, who recounts the atrocities committed by the Guatemalan government against her own family. This remarkable poem is testimony in itself to Harris' belief in the power of poetry to both witness and redeem. (It also, interestingly, offers an implied argument to Erin Mouré's statement in "Seebe" that "The writer as witness, speaking the stories, is a lie, a liberal bourgeois lie. Because the speech is the writer's speech, and each word of the writer robs the witnessed of their own voice, muting them.")

In Harris' poem, it is for the genuine values of the private life — the possibility of love, security, happiness — that the public battle is fought. The "private" life is what makes us human and the poignant hope for its redemption from public violence is what keeps us human. It is unwise, perhaps, in these cynical times to assert with such conviction the possibility of love under such killing circumstances, love *in extremis*. It is also courageous. "Where the Sky is a Pitiful Tent" examines the traditionally-held view of the conservatism of women in the revolutionary context — their holding back, holding on to the personal — and sees in it the source, the very centre of the desire to fight. Rebellion means the end of spiritual death. While, in these conditions of extreme repression, the individual's death is inevitable, so is the courage to continue. The terrible deaths of those who rebel become a vindication of their humanity.

Harris takes on in this poem nothing less than the rediscovery, the reclamation of our own humanity. Her willingness to face our deepest contradictions makes her a poet to whom our deepest attention must be paid.

What is it about ELISABETH HARVOR'S work that makes it so original? She is doing something with poetry I have never seen before, something absolutely new. As a writer of fiction as well as poetry, she approaches narrative with a complete assurance which allows her to manipulate narrative elements in an infinitely flexible manner. A multiple, layered reality which conventional story rarely admits is proposed from this flexible matrix.

In Harvor's work we have the fullness of narrative context without the constraints such a context usually implies. The richness of visual and narrative detail in these poems gives them a filmic quality. Harvor cuts from scenario to scenario, from landscape to portrait to detail with ease and fluidity. But perhaps the deconstructive potential of collage, with its implied breakup of the unitary picture plane, is a better metaphor for Harvor's body of work. The elements of story are there, but they are present in a subversive manner which puts into question the assumptions of naturalistic fiction.

Just as Borson's vision grants a life of their own to the animals, natural elements — even the furniture that inhabits her poetry — Harvor's vision grants for her own images and metaphors an independent life. The narrative in "Saturday Afternoon at the Clinic" moves so forcefully into the Monet and Van Gogh reproductions on the clinic wall that it is only with an effort that we gather ourselves out of the world of the reproductions and back into the presumably dominant reality of the primary narrative.

The building block of Harvor's poetic structure is the long, parenthetical, inclusive sentence which reproduces the parenthetical, inclusive motion of the narrative line. A typical Harvor sentence has modifying phrase hung upon modifying phrase. This clausal, grammatical dependence is an assertion of the causal dependence among people and things; an assertion of connectedness, of interrelationship. The motion of the poem is of wheels within wheels, a circling and circling back reminiscent of the poetic structure underlying both Mouré and Wallace's work (although not the style or voice). This parenthetical movement, its interruptions and interpolations so like female talk, cuts against the grain, the linear drive of traditional narrative. It is an opening up of new possibilities of meaning that interrogates acknowledged reality. We are allowed the story within the story, and the story behind that, and the one behind that one.

Perhaps the most satisfying element of Harvor's poetry is the incredible richness of her voice, its humour, its irony, the range of mood and tone she so easily encompasses. I find Harvor's work (like Mouré's and Paulette Jiles') excessive in the positive sense that it disrupts and exceeds our expectations of writing. We get always more than we bargained for, more than we dared hope for. Harvor's project is to honour the female body, its functions, its joys, even its illnesses. This validation of the body's pleasures is tempered, in many poems, by a rueful perspective on the youthful bravado that takes for granted the body's physical "reliability" and an implied acknowledgement of mortality. Harvor redefines sexuality for us, and the pervasive sexuality of her poetry, its multifaceted eroticism, is one of the defining features of her work. So many women writers remain shackled by the demands of the male gaze. It is still rare, therefore, to see this kind of openness, honesty and integrity in the depiction of the pleasures and dangers of being female, of childbirth and childrearing, of heterosexual love. Harvor is far from blind to the political implications of these dangers. Her poem "In the Hospital Garden" is a fascinating study of (among other things) passivity — an almost voluptuous longing for passivity, for participation in our own destruction, a (mainly) youthful longing for ruin which is masked by the allure, the romanticism of the modern. Harvor's observations on this aspect of sexuality (which is common to both men and women) are frightening but also psychologically authentic.

In addition to this richness of content, Harvor's technical accomplishment enables a tremendous wealth of formal strategies among the various poems. In "At the Horse Pavilion," for example, the entire poem is written as one headlong, breathless sentence. The connective "and," as well as the enjambed (run-on) line breaks, create a tremendous momentum which drives the poem to its conclusion. And in "Saturday Afternoon at the Clinic," Harvor loads the single word "only" with such a multiplicity of meaning it becomes a world, becomes supercharged with signification.

Amplitude seems the best word to describe Harvor's inclusive, unflinching vision, a vision which simultaneously questions our world view and creates it anew.

My first encounter with PAULETTE JILES' work was listening to her read "Going to Church." The poem was so funny, and the female bondage it portrayed so infuriating, that I laughed till I cried and I wanted to cry because I was so mad. When I heard her read the spectacular "Song to the Rising Sun," it moved me in the way I thought only great music could move me. I remember walking away stunned after the friend I had come with and I had risen to our feet in ovation. Jiles' work continues to have this direct, emotional impact on me.

Whenever I now read these poems, I hear Jiles' voice. (I always hear "Going to Church" in her Missouri dialect.) The qualities of her work are the qualities of the great oratorical tradition of the Bible, with its ties to the oral poetry that preceded our literature. But the experience of hearing Jiles read was not just a response to its rhetorical strengths, but to the excessiveness (in the positive sense that I have spoken of Harvor's poetry) of the work, the sense that everything, that more than everything, happens in these poems. Perhaps this is why their effect is such a holistic one; the reader is being appealed to on all levels of her being — physical, emotional and intellectual.

Even in "Going to Church," by far the earliest poem in this selection, Jiles demonstrates the extraordinary control she has over the modulations of voice. The humour in this piece is not just funny; it has something in mind. When the mother's voice intrudes on the teenage narrator's increasingly rebellious monologue, it's comic but it's also surreal, a jarring intrusion onto and transgression into the established reality of the poem. The poem is broken like this at many moments, some of them funny (like the sudden interpolation of the Sunday school admonitions), some transcendent (like the apparition of the fox). Jiles' discourse, like the Cherokee woman who walks through the poem, is both displaced and immediate. Within it, the innumerable systems, the complex machine of the religious patriarchy begins to break up. The powerful "no" (akin to Harris' schoolgirl's refusal) with which the poem ends is in fact an affirmation, a sign of refusing to acquiesce, an act of rebellion.

"One Sister," one of the poems Jiles wrote specifically for radio, continues this displaced and displacing voice. I started off trying to keep track of the sisters, to get the story straight, to tame it into

23

an identifiable narrative structure. But the story is indeed all wrong; it is no story at all; it is everyone's story. Jiles works to accumulate such meaning into the word "sister" that, by the end of the poem, the meaning simply explodes into the universal. This movement describes yet exceeds the notion of sisterhood (a notion that has come to be in many cases nothing more than a platitude of feminism), as the poem's story becomes the story of our disparate, yet common fate.

Jiles is always, inextricably, political and perhaps the greatest synthesis of her political aims comes in "Song to the Rising Sun." Her terrifying evocation of the wreck of the future from which we must extricate ourselves, of the hundred million tons of sulphur dioxide a year we pour into the ionosphere here is more than terrifying, it is moving. It is moving and it moves us to action precisely because the epic movement of the poem is towards hope, towards the rising of the sun. This is an emotional resonance far beyond the possibilities of the lyric Jiles derides. In spite of the ravaged, exquisite landscape portrayed, in spite of the poem's acknowledgement of the ways in which our human minds pause in darkness, the poem is resonant with hope. This epic poem, like the reborn sun, does recreate us; it makes us believe in the possibility of ourselves.

The Neman is a river in the part of the USSR known as Byelorussia; Lake of Two Rivers lies to the north of Toronto in Algonquin Park. The geographic and the biographical names in ANNE MICHAELS' evocative poetry call difference — another time, another place — into being. Mexican poet Octavio Paz writes that poetry is "the *other voice.* Not the voice of history or of anti-history, but the voice which, in history, is always saying something different." An archaeologist, a geologist of the feeling memory, Michaels mines natural history, her own history and the history of our times. For those of us whom history has not treated kindly, the burden of memory is a special one. We are charged with remembering not a world that has passed away, but one that was brutally eradicated. Michaels' work insists on remembering intelligently, remembering in depth; on seeing the present not merely as the present but as the accumulation of the past. She insists also on the three-dimensionality of narrative, its existence in this deep time as well as in place and character.

The use of historical and geographical names functions in the same way in both Michaels' biographical and autobiographical poems. Names work to place the poems within the time-place matrix of history and propose a factuality that is always at issue. By asserting the factual in the imagined, Michaels asserts that any "reality" must be created in the imagination. The fecund reality that Michaels proposes holds both treasure and terror. In Michaels' lyric narratives, the story, like the mother's story in "Lake of Two Rivers," tangles in the wealth, the multiplicity of memory. In this poem, Michaels recounts the fables of her childhood, creating a forceful interplay of narratives, an elision of time and place, of fictitious and factual stories. Details of plot are intricately interwoven with her subjective transformation of events. Michaels does keep her work grounded on a single plane of reality; there is no interplay of textual realities as is found in Harvor's work. However, the reality portrayed is richly conditional to the processes both of history and the imaginative transfiguration of history. The factual events of the narrative are as much a foil as a grounding for the poetic events which are the heart of the work.

Michaels' fascination with time and memory is, like Wallace's, a fascination with mortality. Unlike the child afloat in the continuous present, the adult must acknowledge, however reluctantly, mortality, and so must be aware of the reality of the past, of the future, of time itself and of its implications. The spectacular elegy, "Miner's Pond," is a meditation on this understanding, and on the limits of our understanding. Memory is crucial not only to understanding, but to the survival of the human.

Memory hurts, however, because it reminds us, as Michaels demonstrates in "What the Light Teaches," not only of loss but of the unbearable. Thus memory is also, paradoxically, what must be withstood, what one must be delivered from, because the past can break violently, volcanically into the present. Language can thus be painful too, as the repository of memory. For those who have been displaced by history — whether it be the diaspora, the holocaust, or the Stalinist purges — language can become a country, can become the lost homeland. Through it, memory can uphold the names of our dead, can prove solace against the homesickness of exile. And it is in this way that fear can be translated into love.

Michaels is another poet, like Glickman, whose keenness of intellect and technical accomplishment are matched by depth of emotional perception. The integrity of Michaels' intense, sensuous voice carries the dense, nuanced language gracefully so that the meaning breaks forcefully through.

I heard ERIN MOURÉ read her work before I ever read it on the page. The impact of that reading has stayed with me for the dozen or so intervening years. What struck me then, what strikes me still, is her voice, which I hear always as a physical voice. It is one I find unutterably unique. Mouré is a poet who has the strength to be entirely herself. Her early work (of which "Jump Over The Gate" is an example) had a freshness and vitality that had an immediate and salutary effect on the writing community. While many of us were struggling with The Poetic Voice, that neutral, genderless, classless, bodiless voice of the canon of literature, Mouré was producing texts that provided a paradigm of the individual voice, of voice as the expression of an acknowledged subjectivity. Though it was, in fact, nothing like ordinary speech, the language of her poetry had the authenticity of common parlance. It was and remains entirely un-"poetic" and nonderivative.

The effect of the conventions of The Poetic Voice, which pro-
posed a simplistic, unitary vision of reality, was to limit what was
allowed to happen in the poem. What the poem could contain was
confined to a reflection of the unified, monolithic reality.
Challenging this convention has been another consistent feature
of Mouré's work. "Jump Over The Gate" posits simultaneous real-
ities that interrogate each other; in this case the reality of what we
wish for (Trix's presence) and thereby almost create is opposed to
what our mother tells us (the dog is dead!) and we thereby know
to be true . . . In this early poem, the strength of the subjective,
wished-for reality is both moving in its evocation of loss and scary
in its distance from the objective reality acknowledged at the end
of the poem. The overwhelming power, the conviction of the sub-
jective in Mouré's work can, in poems of this era, border on dislo-
cation, on dissolution.

While the strength of her subjective vision is a constant, Mouré
has moved from the expression of subjectivity to the investigation,
the exploration and evaluation of subjectivity, the questioning of
the unquestioned, static self. While this investigation is informed
by a highly articulated theoretical structure, it has, oddly enough,
a natural quality to it, as though it were a natural predisposition, as
though it were an inevitable drive within the make-up of her mind.

While many poets have been influenced by post-modern and
deconstructivist theory, Mouré, along with Harvor and Harris, seems
particularly capable of incorporating theory into her work in an
integrated manner. She is an active and interested participant in the
current discussion of theory, but her take on deconstruction is def-
initely her own. The work, while it is based on language theory, is
subject to and structured according to its own needs, and not the
needs of theory. There is a certain playfulness of attitude in Mouré's
work that allows her to freely take apart the assumptions of the
genre — as well as the readers' assumptions — to see how it all
works. Like Harris (who was, interestingly, Mouré's high school

English teacher!), Mouré's inventiveness is evident not only in the language of her poetry (the challenge to syntax, diction) but in the structure of the poem itself.

Once the repressive energy of convention is broken into, much more is allowed to happen in the poem. The energy which breaks out in these poems is stimulating both for Mouré's readers and her fellow poets.

Take for example the convention of closure, the assumption that the poem is a linear progression which must come to the point, close in on itself and achieve a tidy conclusion about its subject, a neat package the reader can walk away with. Mouré's work, by contrast, is emphatically open. The poems often speak to each other, refer and connect to each other in a manner that emphasizes that the poem is a product of the subjectivity which created it; an emphasis on the poem as *process* rather than *thing*. The paired poems "Fifteen Years" and "Thirteen Years," like "Jump Over the Gate," propose alternate and opposing realities. While "Fifteen Years" is an apparently nostalgic recollection of youth, "Thirteen Years" is the corrective to it, allowing the repressed and painful memory to surge through the "cover" memory. Another poet would have written the first version, re-remembered, and then have discarded the first so the so-called real version could have stood alone. Mouré allows us the fullness of memory, takes us along for the ride — its detours, side trips, its dead ends.

Indeed, the motion of Mouré's poems feels very close to the structure of memory, of thought itself: the circling and circling back, the skips and leaps and loops. By refusing to weed out, Mouré redefines the real, which includes the false as well as the true. She will summon up a world, painting a physical, vivid and full reality with uncanny acuity, and then equally forcefully subvert and challenge this creation. The poem "The Beauty of Furs" creates a satisfyingly complete work whose meaning is then not merely amplified (as the term "glossary" might suggest) but transmuted, exploded by the companion "Site Glossary" poem which follows.

This strategy of enacting and then exploding meaning has a cumulative impact; within a given book (and within Mouré's body of work as a whole) meaning spirals outwards, drawing more and more into the world of the poetry, connecting and reconnecting with other texts and lives. Perhaps what is most striking about this method is its overwhelming honesty. Language can never be transparent, never be *im*mediate rather than mediate, and yet, by acknowledging this mediacy, Mouré goes very far in extending the limits of poetry's ability to reflect in a fuller way the breadth and complexity, the multivalency, of human experience.

The dead, as BRONWEN WALLACE writes, do bear us forward into the future in their fine, accurate arms. The vitality of Wallace's writing continues beyond her tragic death in 1989, at the age of forty-four. Testimony to her influence on and contribution to the writing community has been given in the many tributes made upon her death. Since her death, we dwell on her remarkable generosity of spirit, often forgetting what a ferocious, and sometimes difficult, friend she was. But that fierceness and stubbornness — the side not often referred to — were an important aspect of the talent that drove Wallace to go so far so fast in her writing, and to stick to the stubbborn heart of things.

I remember my annoyance, when I first heard Wallace read (more than a dozen years ago), at her lack of regard for the kind of technical nitty-gritty I was so punctilious about at the time. I also remember *knowing*, despite my irritation at the rough edges, that here was the real thing, that I was listening to a real poet. There was a tough core to her writing, even then, that was unimpeachable, that had an organic integrity that moved it way beyond competence and into the order of poetry that mattered.

Wallace went on to do a very good job of polishing those edges to a fine sheen, but she honed as well the fierce straightforwardness of her writing, which gives off heat, and not just warmth. For the community of poets around her, Wallace, like Mouré, redefined what poetry could do. She took "the ordinary" into a new place for us. Reading through any one of her books leaves you with the feeling of connection you get from a long afternoon of talk with a good friend: that sense of the fullness of communication real discourse gives. Wallace wields the colloquial style in a supple and effective manner that welcomes and addresses the reader with great clarity of purpose, voice and tone.

Wallace's gift for narrative is the heart of her poetry. Story is how the ephemeral is given form. By the movement of identifiable human lives in an identifiable context (a context at once geographical and social), the story is captured. Wallace is, however, a narrative poet with as much concern for the failure of plot as for plot. Her belief in the ability of story to reveal human meaning is tempered by her knowledge of how difficult that meaning is to grasp, how "the facts" tend to align themselves according to the subjectivity of the teller. Thus, in her work, the apparent verisimilitude of story is continually undercut, challenged. While the individuals her poems describe are clearly credible, and their dilemmas thus present moral as well as aesthetic issues, they are not the stable, consistent "characters" of conventional fiction. Wallace's earlier work sometimes circled this instability fearfully, in an anxious manner which succumbed to the drive of narrative for conclusion. In the mature work of her later books, she lets the poem have its head; she includes the possibility of falling through the story, of the story being no longer such a safe place. The structure of a poem such as "The Man with the Single Miracle" is no longer captive to anecdote, but spirals outward in accordance with the basically expansive nature of Wallace's impulse which is to include and include and include.

Wallace's concern with change, with the passage of time, is often expressed as a Proustian desire to capture time and transcend mortality. The real world, as manifested in everyday life, is a mutable, fragile and (therefore) precious thing. The mutability that characterizes the individuals she portrays makes them both vulnerable and worthy of compassion. In this predicament of vulnerability, transience, we can maintain our humanity only through our ability to integrate, to reconcile our past with our present. This is the role memory plays: to preserve the presence of the past, the continuity of the self. Memory is all our mortality offers us.

Much of the compelling appeal of Wallace's work is this investigation; her genuine, almost obsessive need to understand how it is we can act humanely, humanly. Her work often defines the human by the animal, as she does with the grieving cat in "Familiars" or the self-aware, articulate gorilla in "Koko." The implications of the investigation are broadly political as well as individual, as Wallace insists that it is only by knowing the limits of our humanity that we will be able to preserve our humanity.

Wallace's ultimate project, it seems, is to ascertain the human. She does so without ever resorting to abstraction, without ever accepting the restrictive or reductive view. Her poetry achieves clarity without letting go of complexity. In her brief career, she took on more and more amplitude, felt increasingly capable of dealing simply with the complex. What would she have done had she had the years she deserved?

Wallace has described writing as an act of faith. Her work affirms the possibility of grace, of the gratuitous nature of joy, amid transience, amid mortality. This is profound and moving work. We're lucky to have Bronwen Wallace among us.

❖

Looking back on this book, what astonishes is, again, the amplitude of these women's writing, how broadly they have defined their scope, how wide their concerns are, how richly they draw on literary tradition and on our broader world of knowledge. What is remarkable is their courage, how much is accomplished in their poetry, the range, power and inclusiveness of their work. The many long poems represented are evidence of this will to include and include and include, to take in and take on as much as the world has to offer. It is an encouraging sign, and a reason to hope.

❖

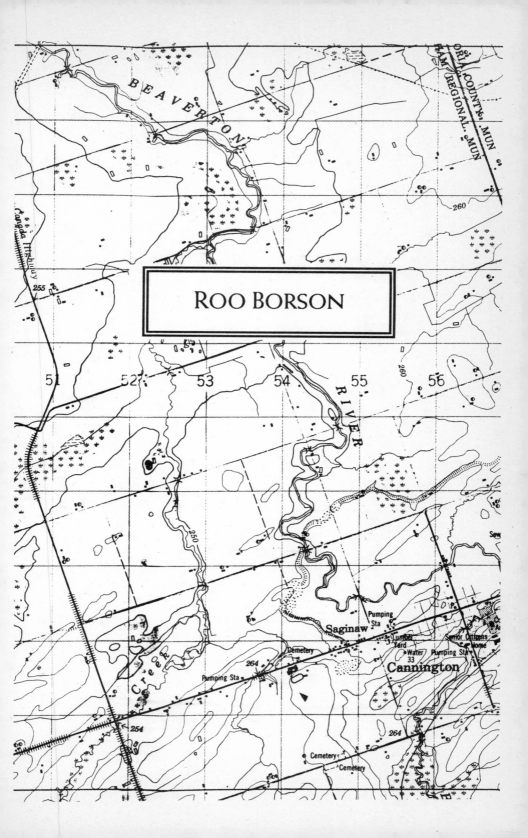

ROO BORSON

— Steven Schwartz

A FEW FIRST PRINCIPLES

"A poet once said, 'The whole universe is in a glass of wine.' We will probably never know in what sense he meant that, for poets do not write to be understood."

— Richard P. Feynman

I WRITE DIRECTLY FROM MY LIFE — from first principles almost, the few givens — life not as story but as moment, i.e. primitively present, in a tactile undiminished world. I exult in the changing weather and mourn too much in advance for whatever will be lost. None of this is intentional. It is a matter of personality. (How strange it is whenever a critic laments that Lowell isn't Bishop or Borges Ondaatje, or vice versa.) But to say something about my writing, let me begin with my reading: I read widely and slowly, pronouncing

each word aloud in my head, rereading the impeccable line or para-
graph over and over sometimes, for the sinuous pleasure of it, then
helplessly forgetting everything but tone. There is something in
me that can't pay attention to plot, but is instantly attuned to colour
and sound, setting, nuance, detail. I learn from other writers, not
through discipline or study, but a curious kind of infatuation.

Experience and language: aren't they — inextricably bound
up together — inescapably elliptical, elusive, allusive? This is the
difficulty in writing, even the forlornness — the resistance of the
medium and its asymptotic frustrations; but it is also the freedom:
since nothing can ever, in some final, monumental sense, be nailed
down or clarified. This means that it is possible to trust in wit, hon-
our the scathing generosity of certain ironists, be welded to the
immovable image, to subversively uphold convention on the whim
(the genius) of the moment. I'm not enough of a believer in poli-
tics to feel dutiful as a writer, to conscientiously assuage, berate, or
shock. But I delight in the huge tireless conversation of literature
— the gossip, the jokes, the revelations, the debate .... That is what
I want to take part in. Spoken song is my medium, and it is proba-
bly my limit.

What I love best in literature are the breathtaking changes of
scale that hint at the larger context: the leaves suddenly alive with
animistic presences; the light solidified on the cheek of one who is
dying; the disembodied, highly embellished and speculative voice
abruptly a million miles away from the claustrophobic, centred lit-
tle human drama so effortlessly dispatched to an inner circle of hell;
even a shift in grammar can set us free. Experience incites language,
but language remembers less securely than the senses, and is there-
fore more alive: it regularly produces marvelous sports, deviations
eerily beyond one's range of style or capacity for thought.

Feynman, a great iconoclast and physicist, perhaps misunder-
stood — or maybe he mistook the bountiful nonlinearity of the
craft for deliberate abstruseness. Maybe he completely missed the

point; or maybe he got it, but wanted to make another.

In the Graduate Reading Room of the Suzallo Library at the University of Washington, the words Poetry and Science are carved side by side in stone above the door. How strange that in my life I've gone in and out only one side of that metaphorical door. Predilection and chance sometimes combine so compellingly we're tempted to call the result talent or destiny. I always write to be understood. I write what I see. The shapeliness of the seeing is what makes the writing speak. Like pure science, the *desire* to speak is based on an overexcitable, irrevocable love of the physical world. I keep thinking of Lorca who, if I remember correctly, once said that if he had been a great poet — that is, capable — he would have written of the sea.

❖

BIOGRAPHICAL NOTE

Roo Borson was born January 20, 1952 in Berkeley, California, and immigrated to Canada in 1974. She received degrees from Goddard College (BA) and the University of British Columbia (MFA). She has given readings and workshops across Canada and in the United States, and has appeared in major anthologies on both sides of the border; she has won prizes in the CBC Literary Competition, twice for poetry and once for nonfiction, and has been nominated for a Governor General's Award; selections of her work have been translated into several languages. She works closely with poet Kim Maltman, and is a member of the group Pain Not Bread. She lives in Toronto.

SNOWLIGHT ON THE NORTHWOOD PATH

Last night on our way to the bathroom after making love
the neighbour's house lights must have stolen
a little way through the kitchen window; as we passed,

the two white bentwood chairs I had brought
with me from Vermont and another life
glowed with a faint, ulterior, mineral half-life —

illusion of a snowed-in night without moon in Vermont.
As once, after a convivial late night with friends,
my companion and I stepped out to a world

not as we'd left it; for while we drank and talked,
obliviously, snow had been falling,
and it had grown clear again, and very cold,

so that the ground glowed, risen several inches.
We weren't dressed for it,
yet chose to walk back by way of the woods,

whose paths, muddled of late by too much use,
had been obliterated by snow, so that we sank
deeper at each step, laughing.

Last night on our way back through the kitchen,
after the brightness of the bathroom, our eyes would not adjust;
the chairs had melded with the dark, and we stumbled.

Yet back in bed as I turned toward sleep
the paths became confused again,
my former life drifting across our life:

I was young, half-dreaming,
and because I had no past to speak of I went forward,
into a cold so extreme

it was at the same time exotically warm —
as though there were no way to distinguish
between the pleasure and the ache,

or to choose, last night,
in the after-ache of pleasure,
between my life and my life.

INTERMITTENT RAIN

Rain hitting the shovel
leaned against the house,
rain eating the edges
of the metal in tiny bites,
bloating the handle,
cracking it.
The rain quits and starts again.

There are people who go into that room in the house
where the piano is and close the door.
They play to get at that thing
on the tip of the tongue,
the thing they think of first and never say.
They would leave it out in the rain if they could.

The heart is a shovel leaning against a house somewhere
among the other forgotten tools.
The heart, it's always digging up old ground,
always wanting to give things a decent burial.

But so much stays fugitive,
inside,
where it can't be reached.

The piano is a way of practising
speech when you have no mouth.
When the heart is a shovel that would bury itself.
Still we can go up casually to a piano
and sit down and start playing

the way the rain felt in someone else's bones
a hundred years ago,
before we were born,
before we were even one cell,
when the world was clean,
when there were no hearts or people,
the way it sounded
a billion years ago, pattering
into unknown ground. Rain

hitting the shovel leaned against the house,
eating the edges of the metal.
It quits,
       and starts again.

WE'RE OUT WITH THE NIGHT BEINGS

We're out with the night beings,
pale airborne zig-zags,
the staggered race through headlights,
once or twice a coyote,
the colour of straw, as ragged,
beings that cross us always from left to right,
barely missed by windshield or tires,
identified by stripe or snout or size
or not at all.
It was in Truth Or Consequences, New Mexico
we tried to stop,
after a rained-out rodeo, local festivities.
Finally found a room, though there was trouble
with a missing key. Unlocked the door to a boy
sitting up suddenly drunk in the dark
on a bed we had bought for the night.
He's not the kind to hurt you, said the desk clerk,
who was also a mother and mistress to a small silent dog
in a rhinestone collar, from behind a display
of earrings on a dead cholla branch,
and anyway he's gone.
We were tired, but took our money and moved on,
because we could,
not sentenced to that town,
we thought, as the boy was, probably for life.
We moved on
with the night beings from the other world,
which is also our world,
with speed and inattention,

42

one of those beautiful emptying hand puppets
now and then by the roadside,
"Guernica," as Klee might have painted it, for a windshield,
through desert where motels grow
arid and square with names like The Sands and Oasis.

POEM BEGINNING WITH A LINE BY
ANNE MICHAELS

I cry for my father because of everyone's short sleeves.
Because of legs and the solemn, thoughtless act of walking.
Because shops are full of goods and they keep ordering more.
Because there is a new kind of metal,
and ties still hang in closets,
and it is Tuesday.
Because of the existence of books,
of boxer shorts, and fedoras, and baseball season,
which will begin again.
Because "dust" is a euphemism
and "cremains" is a new noun
that wasn't in the old dictionary,
because they fit into a gold box the size of a Steuben sculpture.
Because "ashes" is a euphemism
and the box is unexpectedly heavy
and California is flooded
and the fragments are in the rain.
Because bone is variously tubular and spongy
and glows in the dark.
Because it is edible and can be read by.
Because it is possible to throw away someone's false teeth
but not their glasses.

AFTER A DEATH

Seeing that there's no other way,
I turn his absence into a chair.
I can sit in it,
gaze out through the window.
I can do what I do best
and then go out into the world.
And I can return then with my useless love,
to rest,
because the chair is there.

THE THINKER, STONE ORCHARD

Sunflowers' thick stems twisted over, wild yellow curls around the heavy heads, and paired leaves hunched behind like the shoulder-blades of "The Thinker," those poised scales that weigh one thing against another, weigh bronze against air and find them equal, though never balancing. The sunflowers stoop toward summer's end. Nearby, sunrays burn in and out of the copper eyes of a frog, hanging stiff as a little drowned man in the water. Kim, as on all other afternoons, bent over a problem, something with equations, which he spreads across the page, looking between them for the lost error. His shoulders still balancing one thing against another. He loves me. Life will not last.

On the far side of the house two cats roll in sunshine in the catnip patch — they would roll there forever if catnip didn't work its hazy forgetful pleasures — and then they stalk off, stiff-legged, drunkards. Not a yard away, in shadow, the weeds sprout their ragged hearts. The dark part of the garden, left to go to seed — smoky moth, spider in a gauzy net. The place everyone's eye passes over as it makes its rounds. The blind spot. Where everything we do not care to look at lives.

Nighttime, summer countryside. Insects sticking like magnets to the lit screens of the house. In the dark garden it's like standing at the weedy bottom of a well, staring straight up. Kim's shoulders with that athletic tension in them that never gives out. Not just some. All the stars.

After ten afternoons Kim has found the error and moved on, engrossed again. Boxcars of an almost endless train in the distance, metal grumbling about being next to metal. Beyond the mown fields, web of trees, down along the railbed the grey, glinty-eyed rocks, full of frozen forms. Faint moon, exactly torn in half.

SAVE US FROM

Save us from night,
from bleak open highways
without end, and the fluorescent
oases of gas stations,
from the gunning of immortal
engines past midnight,
when time has no meaning,
from all-night cafés,
their ghoulish slices of pie,
and the orange ruffle on the
apron of the waitress,
the matching plastic chairs,
from orange and brown and
all unearthly colours,
banish them back to the test tube,
save us from them,
from those bathrooms with a
moonscape of skin in the mirror,
from fatigue, its merciless brightness,
when each cell of the body stands on end,
and the sensation of teeth,
and the mind's eternal sentry,
and the unmapped city
with its cold bed.
Save us from insomnia,
its treadmill,
its school bells and factory bells,
from living-rooms like the tomb,
their plaid chesterfields

and galaxies of dust,
from chairs without arms,
from any matched set of furniture,
from floor-length drapes which
close out the world,
from padded bras and rented suits,
from any object in which horror is concealed.
Save us from waking after nightmares,
save us from nightmares,
from other worlds,
from the mute, immobile contours
of dressers and shoes,
from another measureless day, save us.

LEAVING THE ISLAND

And then approaches the last ferry, our antics die down, and we wait quietly, if a little reluctantly, but tired and ready, for we are not perpetual motion machines, as the ferry glides in for that random thud, wood against wood, the signal that we can board. Or we could board, except for the uniformed gentleman who, every twenty minutes, back and forth from the mainland, holds departing and prospective passengers at bay, with great ceremony, and finally, at his pleasure, unhooks the rope.

Engine, captain, lifebuoys aside, the essence of the ferry is wood, which floats upon water, and whose varnished grain, in the last rays, gives off such homesickness. Homesickness for the forest, for that primeval state which we have just shaken off so that we might return to the city, to a life in which each transaction must be earned and paid for.

The brief return trip is thus imbued with the momentousness of our voluntary parting from what we think of so fondly as our true nature; a willful sacrifice, an anguish indistinguishable from the ease of coming back to a familiar life. At sundown another ship drifts nearby. Music comes from it, and soon there will be dancing. The ship is tiered, lit up like the birthday cake of a prince or a queen as seen from childhood, a childhood in which only what was codified seemed beautiful. For back then we had to build everything up from nothing, ignorant of the means, that the goal might be merely to reach these very moments in which we flirt with the impulse to demolish all. That foolish notion of courage. And yet finally our image of happiness is complete, insatiable! To live it all again, but this time with full consciousness, *saturated* with consciousness.

STARTING THE TAPE

for David McFadden

After we'd made it through the aerobics section and the endurance
section and the stretches, our teacher reminded us that today was
relaxation day, she switched off the lights and we lay down against
the pitch-dark of our closed eyes, in free-fall really, but kept afloat
in this world by the special exercise floor which had cost the county
taxpayers dearly (it was worth it of course, since it was no mere
floor but a raft of salvation) and our teacher started the tape. I heard
her lie down too as we breathed out and out and the voice on the
tape guided us along, but instead of repeating to myself with each
exhalation the intended phrase I could think only *Il Vecchio is our
love*, over and over, and it worked as well as anything, I felt my indi-
viduality disengage from me, and with it its hobo's sack of joys and
troubles, which was really an old handkerchief knotted to a stick,
the very one presented to me by two long-ago best friends as I set
off on my first trip east and which I still keep, minus the stick, neatly
folded in the top drawer. I experienced the tension in the buttocks,
thighs, and feet, and then the smoothing out, felt myself tacking
toward an approximation of perfection achieved only by ball bear-
ings manufactured in space under near-gravityless conditions, and
I sensed the others nearby, their corresponding stillnesses, as we
lay randomly aligned along the singular plane of the aerobics floor,
as nearly identical as we can be in this life.

Lying there I recalled many things, strands, as it were, of the
softly playing music ... the afternoon a nostalgic chef in Vancouver,
exiled from whichever Old Country he had fled under duress, con-
cocted a fruit omelet in honour of our love; my jewelry box full of
irreparable wrist watches; a single moment of inexcusable cruelty
on an afternoon years ago, when I had just finished refilling the
cat's food dish. The cat was sick, as it turned out, nearly unto death,

50

and continued to stand howling mechanically beside it, until, in vexed helplessness, I grasped the back of his head and turned it, saying, uselessly, and lowering myself in my own estimation as I did so, *Look, food, eat it*. After a moment's pause he went on as before, weeping pitiably at the ceiling, because he had to, his hunger was for no mortal food.

I was breathing in and in now, silently pronouncing *I'm full of energy*, but in a tone of irony the voice on the tape could never condone, when it came to me that a sense of irony is merely the rebellion of the still-young-at-heart, which could only mean that I was more full of energy than I had admitted. After class I went home and continued reading a book of poems called *Gypsy Guitar* until it was time for the news. It seemed the writers' strike had ended, and the poker-faced buffoon whom the news team had rewarded with a short spot on the subject declared, in the end, "Let's face it: we live in a thirty- to forty-channel world," and for him that seemed to sum it up.

IT'S RAINING

A rich rain is falling and my mother is nowhere to hear it.
Bells, bells, bells — thunder's huge
omniscient wheels passing over us.
But we with our thoughts are
not crushed, surely.
Only the dog is, ears flat,
shivering where he lies.

BIBLIOGRAPHY (SELECTED)

Landfall. Frederiction: Fiddlehead Poetry Books, 1977.

In the Smoky Light of the Fields. Toronto: Three Trees Press, 1980.

Rain. Moonbeam: Penumbra Press, 1980.

A Sad Device. Dunvegan: Quadrant, 1981.

Night Walk [chapbook]. Toronto: Missing Link #3, 1981.

The Whole Night, Coming Home. Toronto: McClelland & Stewart, 1984.

With Kim Maltman. *The Transparence of November/Snow*. Kingston: Quarry Press, 1985.

Intent, or the Weight of the World. Toronto: McClelland & Stewart, 1989.

ANTHOLOGIES

Atwood, Margaret, editor. *The New Oxford Book of Canadian Verse*. Toronto: Oxford University Press, 1982.

Bennett, Donna & Brown, Russell, editors. *An Anthology of Canadian Literature In English*. Vol. II. Toronto: Oxford University Press, 1983.

Callahan, Barry, editor. *Lords of Winter and of Love*. Toronto: Exile Editions, 1983.

LaDuke, Janice & Luxton, Steve, editors. *Full Moon*. Dunvegan: Quadrant Editions, 1983.

Norris, Ken, editor. *Canadian Poetry Now, 20 Poets of the '80's*. Toronto: Anansi, 1984.

di Michele, Mary, editor. *Anything Is Possible, A Selection of Eleven Women Poets*. Oakville: Mosaic, 1984.

Janeczko, Paul B., editor. *Pocket Poems*. New York: Bradbury Press, 1985.

Lee, Dennis, editor. *The New Canadian Poets 1970-1985*. Toronto: McClelland & Stewart, 1985.

Hunter, J. Paul, editor. *The Norton Introduction to Poetry*, 3rd Edition. New York: Norton, 1986.

Chester, Laura, editor. *Deep Down, the New Sensual Writing by Women*. New York: Faber & Faber, 1988.

Allen, Robert, editor. *The Lyric Paragraph*. Montreal: DC Books, 1988.

Nemiroff, Greta, editor. *Celebrating Women: Poetry and Short Stories by and about Canadian Women*. Toronto: Fitzhenry and Whiteside, 1989.

Sullivan, Rosemary, editor. *Poetry by Canadian Women*. Toronto: Oxford, 1989.

Charlesworth, Roberta A. & Lee, Dennis, editors. *A New Anthology of Verse*. Toronto: Oxford, 1989.

Scheier, Libby, Sheard, Sarah, & Wachtel, Eleanor, editors. *Language in Her Eye: Writing and Gender*. Toronto: Coach House Press, 1990.

The Norton Introduction to Literature, 5th Edition. New York: Norton, 1991.

The Norton Introduction to Literature, Shorter. New York: Norton, 1991.

The Norton Introduction to Poetry, 4th Edition. New York: Norton, 1991.

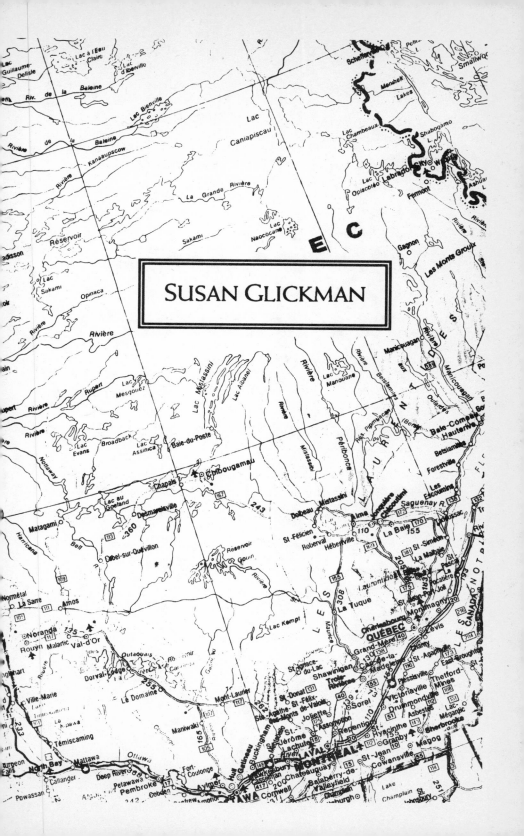

BUT WHY POETRY?

MY FOUR-YEAR-OLD NEPHEW telephoned me recently to ask "Auntie Susan, why is 'shampoo' called 'shampoo' when there's no poo in it?" My appreciative laughter was almost drowned out by his exuberance at having made such a good joke — this despite the fact that he doesn't know the word "sham" and therefore didn't realize *how* good the joke *was*! Eventually I told him that in India, where the term "shampoo" comes from, it doesn't have a funny sound like it does here, and that satisfied his curiosity. But it didn't diminish our mutual pleasure in the game of language.

For me, this is where poetry begins; not necessarily with bad puns, but always with appreciation for the sounds, rhythms, and connotations of words. So when people ask me, as they often do at readings, "When did you start writing poetry?" I just reply that it's not a question of starting, it's just that poets, unlike most people, never stop.

On the other hand, the American poet James Wright said somewhere "the kind of poetry I want to write is the poetry of a grown man." Well, I'm not a man, and I'm not "grown," but these reservations aside I share his goal. Play may be the work of childhood, but a more serious commitment is required of those who choose poetry as a vocation. What makes *adult* poetry, I think, is a sense of the complexity of being in time (and of being a being in one's particular times). History has to come in, and politics, the dirt under people's nails, their fists, their tenderness.

For women, whose lives have too often been shrouded in silence, this project has a special urgency. To attend to women's lives as if they mattered — as if the daily business of half the world counted for something — is something I try to do in my own work. And to do so is necessarily to unlearn inhibitions and reject prescriptions about what constitutes "poetic" material and whose voice is empowered to speak. Every poem involves a little dance between convention and improvisation, a negotiation for integrity. Like all traditional women's occupations it's work that goes largely unacknowledged and is never done.

This is why I don't consider myself "grown," to reprise Wright. To envision oneself as, in some way, finished, to impose closure, is a failure of the imagination. Individual poems may end but poetry does not. Poetry is a form of discovery which both observes and participates in the process of becoming; if it teaches us anything it is the multivalency of our experience. A single moment of feeling/thinking/perceiving can be almost inexhaustable, and bafflingly full of contradictions. Perhaps this is why I enjoy puns so much — they're the verbal equivalent of how the world feels to me.

So the poetry that pleases me best, while adult in its engagement with experience, still has something of a child's delight in the enchanted weirdness of language. The medium is never purely transparent; we don't *see through* language to "reality" but create a fictional reality, however tenuous, by the language we use. It has texture and colour; it grunts and sighs; we build stuff with it.

Any craft is a lifelong discipline, requiring respect for one's materials and an attention amounting, sometimes, almost to trance. How slowly one learns the sinews and joints of language, articulating its body with gesture and voice and breath! But how profound the pleasure when the line sings so one's nerves vibrate in sympathy! This is why I don't buy the current version of the Eden myth made fashionable by Lacan: that the acquisition of language results in a body/mind split betraying some prelapsarian infantile union with the cosmos. Far from being externally imposed, the drive to language appears to be innate. Even when there are no signing adults around to imitate, deaf babies "babble" as enthusiastically with their hands as hearing ones do with their mouths. There's a large area of our brains devoted just to language; anatomically, we're better evolved for talking to each other than we are for walking upright.

But why poetry? Because we don't just want to walk, we want to dance! We need more than exercise, we need to express and interpret the world around us. And poetry, as I suggested before, is a form of rapt attention which, in its double focus on world and word, helps to sharpen both. Sharp things hurt more, but they also shine. And you can see yourself in them.

❖

BIOGRAPHICAL NOTE

Susan Glickman was born in 1953 and grew up in Montreal. She has studied, worked and traveled in many countries, including Greece, England, the United States, India and Mexico. After working in publishing, she did a PHD in Renaissance drama, and now teaches at the University of Toronto. She is currently working on a study of the representation of landscape in Canadian poetry.

HENRY MOORE'S SHEEP

for Bronwen Wallace

NOTE

In 1972 Henry Moore dedicated his "Sheep Notebook" to his daughter. Published by Thames and Hudson (New York, 1980), it is a record of Moore's growing interest in, and affection for, the sheep grazing on his estate.

I

The first page of the notebook reads:

> Subjects — insects
> Tadpoles   Sheep
> Birds
> labyrinth

and whirring like moths   in lamblight

quick-wriggling in spring

melodious bleaters

amazing they are all

simply *Sheep* !

II

Page after page these
blunt-faced grazers, impassive as slippers;
heads wedges of darkness surrounded by barbed-wire.
Nature's doodles, scrawled with one hand
while the mind invents

heron
        apricot

                lotus

all things articulate and elegant.

Clownlike and tedious, their lumpen assertion
of mere presence.
As we expect.
As in "they're all a bunch of sheep."
As in the mob to which we most certainly do not
belong, being
if not elegant
at least strenuous pursuers of some moral or aesthetic
   imperative unattributable to mutton at the mall
or at the polls
or to anything en masse except (perhaps)
hillsides spread with some purposeful flower
nature has provided to replenish our weary spirits
and to remind us that she deserves time off

after all

    for small amusements

       like sheep.

III

And then sheepishly, Henry
acknowledges their right to be,
to be there, in spring, dirty wet coats in the long green grass.

Insatiable.
        Mild.
                Happy.

Symbols of nothing but themselves —
their placid appetite an astonishment
to everything worried
or fierce.
And then he looks again.

And he sees the sheep have dark intelligent eyes; they regard him
without alarm but with a strange intensity.
He pencils this in.

Then he notices the long and lovely sweep of bone from forehead
to nose, and gives the skull
definition. The ears and tail emerge
from fur, the tail an extra limb
more expressive than any penis, and he thinks
I have nothing like this
and suddenly envies the sheep.

It only takes a few pages.
And when he starts envying the sheep
they become female.
Those dormant blobs rouse themselves, heat rises from the page:
their bodies urge on the urgent suckling lambs
their tails beat time to the
pure unblushing springtime tra-la,
the hungers and loves
of sheep.

IV

Sheep sheep

lambs/ sheep
sheep

sheep / lambs

sheep/lambs

Henry's notebook records
the holy families
of the fields.

V

And this is the strange part —
his sheep are more motherly
than his women.
They're all good sports in comfortable clothes
who never lose their tempers or
lament their figures.
They are playful and rueful and funny
and have the intelligence that comes
with love.

What is it about Moore's women?
Why do his women have less wit
than his sheep?

Great bleached pelvic sculptures.
Womb-hollowed matriarchs immobilized before
tall buildings, prone before the phallic etcetera towers
of modern commerce to whose gods they are spread
as sacrifice bare on the pavement.
Moore's women are the caryatids
of capitalist temples — every bank
needs one; every corporation can satisfy share-holder
and tax-man with a plaza full of Mama.

Earthbound, wide-hipped and heavy stomached,
balanced on haunches or elbows, propped on spindley arms,
    with small heads and pinpoint eyes, thin-lipped smiles;
anacephalic, myopic, and gross.
Or bone ladies, ghosts of childbearing past.
Either way oppressed, and oppressive.
Either way, the body
as a terrible sadness.

VI

If tragic, then heroic?
But still
body   body   body
organizing the space around it into
background, asserting presence
not relationship
past and future nullified in the moment's
insistence.

Even in the dyads
of mother and child there is this
isolation.
In the family groups each member looks
a different way;
each gaze pins a separate
vanishing point.

VII

How to account for this contrast?

The pastoral theme, perhaps, that old lie about *The Fall* —
Eve withdrawn into her sad mortality
and the curly ignorant sheep, O happy happy sheep
forever panting and forever young?

Or but a formal contingency, structural support
being required for sculpture — hence she's recumbent
in four dimensions while they frolic freely
in two?

Or what's Mo(o)re personal, implied
by the analogy, analogy by its nature
implying both likeness and difference.
As thus:
        the lambs are seen
        from the parent's perspective, the women
        from a child's point of view:
        Big Momma and little me.

So his tenderness goes to the sheep
and his ambivalence to
the human figures.

It figures.

VIII

Henry, not that you did wrong, but that you said so well
what we had heard for too long without hearing, the old rhymes:

womb/tomb

death/breath

bone/stone/moan

mother/other

and therefore made them finally redundant

And for the larger-than-life-size statement of filial guilt
confronting us in the theatre of public places
so that each action reveals its origin
in maternal suffering, its backdrop of maternal compliance
its fountain of mother's milk

For this we thank you

But Henry, there's more sentimentality in these
bronze heroines
than in all your fluffy lambs.

IX

The middle of the notebook is full of sheep
and lambs and lambs and sheep
placidly eating in turbulent fields which
unravel into woods and the woods
into skies tied together with
wool, all one great ecstatic
snarl —

in the cosmology of sheep
everything's connected.

On the last pages of the notebook the sheep
are shorn.
Slack-bellied and heavy-uddered,
the poor, bare creatures
stand stark in that darkness
which defines them

but the oblivious lambs suck on.

BEAUTY

Maybe there are no easy deaths but Grandpa's
was terrible. The scuttling crab-wise crawl
of the disease eating him
for months, a slow insult.
The scotch-and-nicotine smell of him
gone off, festering,
so that even he flinched from his skin,
that strange dank leather
clammy as a wet groundsheet
stretched over his bones.
Bones he'd kept modestly hidden
in his patriarch's bulk, his executive jowls,
all naked and poor
in plain view — my fierce private grandfather
exposed.

My mother was afraid of him:
his *Sit up straight!* his *Girls
don't go to college.*
My sister, only little when he died, remembers
a scowling giant whose moustache spoiled
his kisses.
And he *was* fierce, his longshoreman's fists,
but with me he was always courtly. We discussed things.
And Grandpa, you were right,
which I knew even then, about beauty.
It comes from inside, you said (But I was only
twelve, desperate for power, afraid I might never
have any) *It has nothing to do
with fashion.*

We were sitting in your wood-panelled den, the TV on
to *Bonanza* or *Perry Mason*, your favourites,
and talking. And I knew you were right.
But even now I can feel that hard little knot, that "no,"
stuck in my throat like a candy
stolen from your secret cupboard and swallowed guiltily
and whole, that knot of stubbornness which, like the candy,
like everything I took from you, silver dollars, a complete set
of Dickens, your gold pen, was mine
from inside, my true inheritance.

SILVERPRINT

The leafless tree behind Great Aunt Edna's head is sharply etched as a master drawing but her face, shadowed by the broad-brimmed hat, is sweetly out of focus. She resembles Virginia Woolf, or rather Virginia Stephen; the same swan-necked langour, angularity of jaw, pouting lip. Not smiling, but poised.

My grandmother Dorothy stands in front and to the right of her graceful sister, sway-backed, grimacing into the sun. She's very young, a little chubby and clumsy. They are dressed alike in long buttonless jackets loosely belted over patterned blouses; both wear straw hats trimmed with flowers.

A small gingerbread house with a single chimney completes the picture; Edna leans on a fence. This is New York, 153rd Street, in April of 1919. This is before Dorothy married my grandfather and moved to Montreal and beautiful Edna followed. This is before Grandma taught me casino and gin rummy, took me to movies and let me try on her makeup; before egg creams on Edna's balcony watching heat-lightning over the city. I never saw this picture of them while they were still alive.

This is how I remember them now; two girls in springtime after the Great War. I dust the photograph in an apartment full of their belongings — Edna's table, Dorothy's chairs; Dorothy's pitcher, Edna's clock.

When Grandma was dying I came for a visit from England and she made me go back and died the next day. When Edna was dying I came on a visit from Toronto and she made me go back and died the same week. "Thank you for coming, darling" they both said, and turned away their silver heads.

KODACHROME

Except that Grandma never had silver hair, not in my lifetime. It was dyed red, and even after the chemotherapy she wore a red wig. This was her spiritual if not her natural colour; it went with the raucous laughter, the green eyeshadow, the charm bracelet whose golden trinkets I would lie in bed trying to remember: a tiny loving-cup, a ball studded with pearls, an amber seal engraved with an open pair of scissors.

Edna remained a lady and wore a blue rinse and pastel knit dresses. She made bran muffins and candied almonds and gave me embroidered handkerchiefs for my birthday. Not having children of her own, she took the role of Great Aunt seriously; she assumed the dignity of a grand-parent with none of the attendant emotional confusion.

Once after Grandma died we were home for a holiday, my brothers and sister and I, being a family, filling up the house. For diversion after dinner we played some old tapes and suddenly her voice rang out loud and unexpected as a rock through the living-room window. There was more of her in that voice, more colour, than in any photograph. Nobody knew what to say.

Edna, though, remains a mystery; never more nor less here than in that captured image, April 1919, a shadowy beauty under a broad-brimmed hat. She was so passive and bewildered always; at the mercy of others' good wishes and capable hands. She cried when she knew she was dying because it wasn't fair and she didn't understand. But Grandma — Grandma took charge, shooed us away, pulled off her red wig and was ready to go.

FAMILIES

Once at the breakfast table when that harsh bitching
that passes for a stab but is really more like sawing away
with a rusty breadknife, leaving a jaggedy scar,
passed as usual in those days between my mother
and me my father began to cry
into his cornflakes. Big round tears for the lost family
on the cereal box; the one that was supposed to come
with the yellow breakfast-nook, the apple-tree
out back. Only one tree, our neighbour's, dropping its fruit
over the fence. Generous, but not big enough
to hide in, so there was nowhere to shelter, no option
but escape. But Dad had his job, his car, his sense of humour;
deep down hadn't he always known there *was*
nowhere else to go? That a family only keeps smiling
in photographs and even there
someone's always out of focus. Him, for example;
his eyes inevitably shut, as though caught by chance
between blinks, when really, it was a reflex, like sneezing.
He could smile or keep his eyes open — but not both.

I could make that a metaphor I guess, or quote Tolstoy in
Anna Karenina, but happiness in families is also complex
and not to be sneezed at. The problem is more with the way
we apprehend feelings in time. Sadness is so slow, a mule with
split hooves, picking its way over stone. Joy,
in this ratio, a 40s convertible, his first car,
speeding down green summer roads to a *doo-wap* refrain.
That is, when you're happy you don't have to know all the words,
humming along does just fine. But grief,

grief makes us all precisions, analyzing each other
to death: *You failed me, and this is exactly how*.

Meanwhile the evidence of our honourable if partial success
piles up — all those turkeys, ribbons, pots of flowers.
In their albums the smiles brave out our disregard,
bleaching a little with the years like the cedar dock down
at the lake, that worn path between the house
and the silent water: between what contains the family
and what it keeps them from. Lying on that dock with eyes closed
I told my mother all about you before we were married,
when I still wasn't sure; some of the old harshness in my voice
because I wanted or expected her to tell me not
to do it, to tell me the pains were more real
than the joy. But she didn't. No one could save me from my own
trip down that road; no one wanted to.
And so I jumped off the split grey boards into the reflections
of trees and clouds and swam away very fast from that house
to this one, into a new family. Eyes wide open,
but under water.

ONE

for my nephew Jonathan

"And when I found the door was shut
I tried to turn the handle but."
                    — Lewis Carroll

This is the year you will never remember.
You'll be told about it more often than you can bear; about how
you cried for 4 months, then sat up and grasped
the world. That you could *do* things — not just submit — changed
your disposition: you clutched and crawled
and laughed out loud. Became everyone's darling, who'd been
a holy terror. Oh, you taught us all respect, you
cunning cherub, first
of your generation.
But we'll get our revenge.
We'll tell stories about you, dotingly, over and over,
refining our memories. We'll anatomize you
attributing cheekbone and eyelash and nostril,
forehead and buttock and shoulder
to someone else. We'll distribute your talents impartially
among the needier of our relations
so they can share in your achievements.
We'll say *of course* to everything you do; as in
Of course he's a good athlete! Do you remember
those legs at birth? or
Of course he's moody; remember how he was
those first months?
And you, of course, will be excluded
since this is the year
you will never remember.

81

But what if you could?
What if you could reclaim for yourself, in yourself
what so deeply you awaken in us: this newness?
How the world is before the odd drift of things
congeals into familiarity; before faces, those pinkish blurs
of emotion, stiffen into fixed
identities —
before we assume we know anything at all.
And how it was for you when you started knowing;
we, the adults who pretend to understand you, assume
that was when you stopped crying.
But maybe that was when you started.

And yet again no, no dice, seeing your face so expectant,
so sure that today will be wonderful,
I know the rote skepticism of tired minds doesn't
belong here.
Sitting with you in the grass holding a flower,
the one flower in the world, all there is of yellow
in sunlight, so bright it startles you, you look at me and
seeing me smile, smile back your happy astonishment
that this thing can be here too, this flower you can actually
hold, and the dog who lets you pat her, her soft fur
almost the colour of the flower, you are overcome
and try to clap your hands
and who taught you that?
When I tell you the story will I add that you missed —
not having the co-ordination at 8 months to join palms on cue —
and that I wondered about the relationship of applause
to prayer,
something only you could tell me about, my angel.
But I don't suppose you will, because
this is the year you will never remember.

And then the next time I saw you, three months later,
you were walking — already, it seemed, reconciled to a
new point of view. Such nonchalance, such a swagger
of diapers! Little boy,
the dimensions you move through describe a
higher geometry,
any given point occupying limited space
but infinite time.
Which is why we want to stop you
if only in *our* memories.
You're about to touch down on that thick-aired planet we others
inhabit, where time is always too short
and the compass bewildering.
I just wish you a small reserve of the joy you have now
to go on with, that's all. The rest is best
as mystery, which is why

this is the year you will never remember.

BIBLIOGRAPHY

Complicity. Montreal: Signal Editions, Véhicule Press, 1983.

The Power to Move. Montreal: Signal Editions, Véhicule Press, 1986.

Henry Moore's Sheep, and Other Poems. Montreal: Signal Editions, Véhicule Press, 1990.

ANTHOLOGIES (SELECTED)

LaDuke, Janice & Luxton, Steve, editors. *Full Moon*. Dunvegan: Quadrant Editions, 1983.

di Michele, Mary, editor. *Anything Is Possible, A Selection of Eleven Women Poets*. Oakville: Mosaic, 1984.

Allen, Robert, editor. *The Lyric Paragraph*. Montreal: DC Books, 1988.

Sullivan, Rosemary, editor. *Poetry by Canadian Women*. Toronto: Oxford, 1989.

Nemiroff, Greta, editor. *Celebrating Women: Poetry and Short Stories by and about Canadian Women*. Toronto: Fitzhenry and Whiteside, 1989.

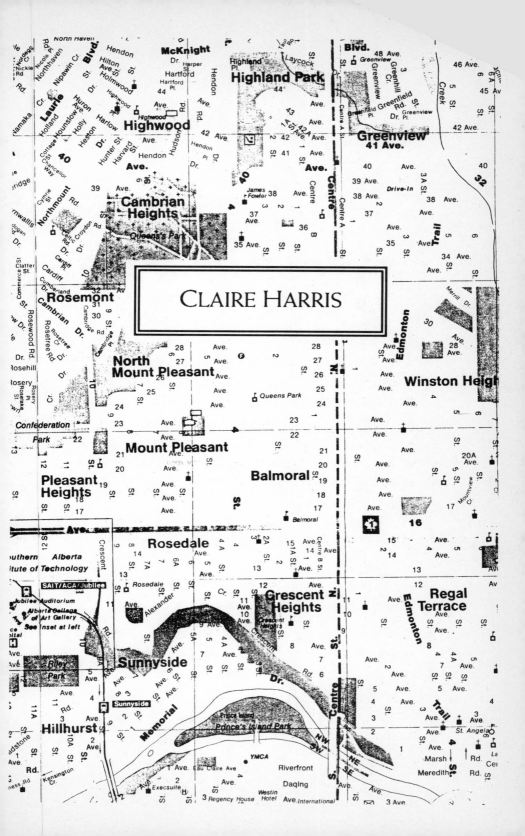

CLAIRE HARRIS

A REAL GOOD LEMONADE

I AM AN AFRICAN DESCENDED from those branded and dragged to the Americas to provide free labour and riches for the West. I am a woman in a world in which full humanity is still understood as not being female. Yet I have chosen to live and write in this society in which race and gender lie at the heart of any definition of nationality. Why? Because in the world over which the West continues to exercise a ruthless hegemony, *real* human beings are European and male. The rest of the race is ranked accordingly. The further from the centre the further from God. So it matters little where I live. At least here I can write without fear of cholera, malaria, outdated and dumped drugs, food, medical and other equipment, and of course, chemical dumping. That is done in the neighbourhoods of the poor. At the moment, I'm not poor. That's hardly surprising. The world economic system is organized and maintained so that the advantages flow overwhelmingly to the West. I suppose it is important to say here how this has affected, first my philosophy, and then my writing.

I have come to understand that the noble ideals of iconic Western humanists, philosophers, even of Western religions, are undermined by their inherent sexism, Eurocentrism, homophobia, and the drive to power through any means. The *all's fair in love, war and capitalism* syndrome. Morality has little to do with the actual life of the West: the thousand daily choices of ordinary existence, and the political, economic, social and emotional decisions which we shape and mythologise into a culture. Given free rein, the folkways of diehard capitalism and power are often catastrophic for those regarded as disposable, as other. Thus I have been freed to choose for myself. To choose consciously. Most people rely for the sense of self on the perceptions of the society in which they find themselves. I know that the perceptions of this society are often both willfully and necessarily false. I have been freed to form my own. This is demanding and somewhat dangerous work. Dangerous to the soul, I mean. More important, it has forced me to ask the question *what does it really mean to be human?* Both in form and content, my poetry is an attempt to respond to that interest. That is why so much of it starts with "factual accounts" of lived experience; why I write both with and against the modernist grain. If my work seems "political," it is because it is. One either supports the status quo, or one doesn't. What is more interesting is that so many seem to be unaware that up to the late nineteenth century much English verse was exactly that, overtly political; if by political we mean that which matters to society as a whole. So political that the writings of women were, on the whole, simply excised.

However, I am not sufficiently the egoist to take upon myself the job of spokesperson for Africans everywhere. Unlike my European counterparts who surely must be speaking for all Europeans, since they are always so surprised to discover that I am not speaking for all Africans. Race and gender are at the heart of any experience, any sense of the self. My writing, therefore, in obvious or subtle ways, naturally reflects both my race, gender, and aspects of the culture I was born to — a quality I share with most if not all writers. One hopes that it will eventually dawn on the larger society that it is possible for me to be Canadian. If it does not, we are doomed to repeat the generally disastrous American experience. That would be a pity.

❖

BIOGRAPHICAL NOTE

Claire Harris came to Canada from Trinidad, West Indies in 1966. She settled in Calgary where she teaches English in the Separate Schools. In 1975, during a leave of absence in Nigeria, she began to write for publication. She was poetry editor of the Alberta quarterly Dandelion from 1981 to 1989. She has been a member of the Writer's Guild of Alberta since its inception. Her first book, Fables from the Women's Quarters, won a Commonwealth Award. Travelling to Find a Remedy won the Writer's Guild of Alberta Award for Poetry and the first Alberta Culture Poetry Prize. In 1990 The Conception of Winter won an Alberta Culture Special Award for poetry.

POLICEMAN CLEARED IN JAYWALKING CASE

The city policeman who arrested a juvenile girl for jaywalking March 11, has been cleared of any wrongdoing by the Alberta law enforcement appeal board. The case was taken to the law enforcement appeal board after the girl was arrested, strip-searched and jailed in the adult detention centre.
The police officer contended the girl had not co-operated during the first five minutes after she was stopped, had failed to produce identification with a photo of herself on it, and had failed to give the policeman her date of birth.

— Edmonton Journal

In the black community to signify indicates an act of acknowledgement of sharing, of identifying with.

The girl was fifteen. An eyewitness to the street incident described her as "terrified."

The girl handed the officer her bus pass containing her name, address, phone number, her school, school address and phone number.

Look you, child, I signify   three hundred years in swarm around me
this thing I must   this uneasy thing   myself the other   stripped
down to skin and sex   to stand   to stand and say   to stand and say
before you all   the child was black and female and therefore mine
listen   you walk the edge of this cliff with me at your peril do not hope
to set off safely to brush stray words off your face to flick an idea off with
thumb and forefinger   to have a coffee and go home comfortably
Recognize this edge   and this air carved with her silent invisible cries
Observe now this harsh world   full of white works   or so you see us
and it is white   white washed male and dangerous even to you full of
white fire white heavens white words   and it swings in small circles
around you   so you see it   and here I stand black and female
bright black on the edge of this white world   and I will not blend in
nor will I fade into the midget shades   peopling your dream

Once long ago   the loud tropic air   the morning rushing by in a whirl
of wheels   I am fifteen drifting through hot streets shifting direction by
instinct   tar heel soft under my shoes I see shade on the other side of the
road   secure in my special dream I step off the curb   sudden cars
crash and jangle of steel   the bump the heart stopping fall into silence
then the distant driver crying "Oh Gawd! somebody's girl child she step
off right in front of me, Gawd!"   Black faces anxious in a fainting world
a policeman bends into my blank gaze   "where it hurting yuh?   tell
me!"   his rough hand under my neck   then seeing me whole "stand
up, let me help yuh!" shaking his head   the crowd straining on the
sidewalk the grin of the small boy carrying my books   then the
policeman   suddenly stern "what you name, girl?"   the noisy separa-
tion of cars   "eh, what you name?" I   struck dumb   dumb
"look child, you ever see a car in plaster of paris?"   dumb   "tell me
what's your name? You ever see a car in a coffin!"   the small boy calling
out my name into such shame   But I was released with a smile   with
sympathy sent on in the warm green morning   Twenty years later to lift
a newspaper and see my fifteen year old self   still dumb   now in a
police car   still shivering as the morning roars past but here   sick in
the face of such vicious intent

Now female I stand in this silence   where somebody's black girl child
jaywalking to school is stripped   spread   searched   by a woman
who finds that black names are not tattooed on the anus pale hands soil-
ing the black flesh   through the open door the voices of men in cor-
ridors   and in spite of this   yea   in spite of this black and female to
stand here and say   I am   she is   I say to stand here   knowing
this is a poem black in its most secret self

Because I fear   I fear myself and I fear your skeletal skin the spider
tracery of your veins   I fear your heavy fall of hair like sheets of rain and
the clear cold water of your eyes   and I fear myself the rage alive in me
consider the things you make even in the mystery of earth and the things
you can   an acid rain that shrivels trees   your clinging fires that
shrivel skin   This law that shrivels children and I fear your naked fear
of all that's different   your dreams of power your foolish innocence
but I fear myself and the smooth curve of guns   I fear   Look   your
terrible Gods do not dance nor laugh nor punish men   do not eat or
drink but stay a far distance   watch the antic play of creation and can-
not blink or cheer   Even I fear the ease you make of living this stolen
land   all its graceful seductions   but I fear most myself   how easy to
drown in your world   dead believe myself living   who stands "other"
and vulnerable to your soul's disease
Look you, child, I signify

WHERE THE SKY IS A PITIFUL TENT

Once I heard a Ladino say "I am poor but listen I am not an Indian," but then
again I know Ladinos who fight with us and who understand we're human beings
just like them.*

— Rigoberta Menchú (Guatemala)

All night the hibiscus tapped at our jalousies
dark bluster of its flower trying to ride in
on wind lacinated with the smell of yard fowl
Such sly knocking sprayed the quiet
your name in whispers
dry shuffle of thieving feet on verandah floors
My mouth filled with midnight and fog
like someone in hiding
to someone in hiding
I said *do not go*
you didn't answer
though you became beautiful and ferocious
There leached from you three hundred years of compliance

*Ladino: Originally descendants of Spanish Jews who came to Guatemala dur-
ing the Inquisition; currently used for any Guatemalan who rejects Indian
values or Mayan origin. Also implies person of mixed heritage.

Now I sleep with my eyes propped open
lids nailed to the brow

After their marriage my parents went into the mountains to establish a small settlement ... they waited years for the first harvest. Then a **patron** *arrived and claimed the land. My father devoted himself to traveling and looking for help in getting the rich landowners to leave us alone. But his complaints were not heard ... they accused him of provoking disorder, of going against the sovereign order of Guatemala ... they arrested him.*

From the testimony of Rigoberta Menchú translated by Patricia Goedicke, American Poetry Review (January/February 1983).

In the dream I labour toward something
glimpsed through fog   something of us exposed
on rock and mewling   as against the tug of water
I struggle under sharp slant eyes
death snap and rattle of hungry wings
                                   Awake I whisper
You have no right to act
you cannot return land from the grave
Braiding my hair the mirror propped on my knees
I gaze at your sleeping vulnerable head
Before the village we nod smile or don't smile
we must be as always
while the whole space of day aches with our nightmares
I trail in your footsteps through cracks you chisel
in this thin uncertain world
where as if it were meant for this mist hides
sad mountain villages   reluctant fields
still your son skips on the path laughing
he is a bird   he is a hare
under the skeletal trees

My mother had to leave us alone while she went to look for a lawyer who would take my father's case. And because of that she had to work as a servant. All her salary went to the lawyer. My father was tortured and condemned to eighteen years in prison. (Later he was released.) But they threatened to imprison him for life if he made any more trouble.

I watch in the market square
those who stop and those who do not
while my hands draw the wool over up down
knitting the bright caps on their own
my eyes look only at sandals
at feet chipped like stones at the quarry
There are noons when the square shimmers
we hold our breath while those others
tramp in the market place
Today the square ripples like a pond
three thrown   what is left of them
corded like wood   alive and brought to flame
How long the death smoke signals
on this clear day
We are less than the pebbles under their heels
the boy hides in my shawl

The army circulated an announcement ordering everyone to present themselves in one of the villages to witness the punishment the guerillas would receive ... There we could observe the terrible things our comrades had suffered, and see for ourselves that those they called guerillas were people from the neighbouring villages ... among them the Catequistas and my little brother ... who was secretary to one of the village co-operatives. That was his only crime. He was fourteen years old ... They burnt them.

As if I have suffered resurrection I see
the way the grass is starred with thick fleshed
flowers at whose core a swirl of fine yellow
lines disappear into hollow stems
so we now into our vanished lives
Dusk thickening trees we turn
to the knotted fist of mountains
clenched against mauve distance
Because I must   I look back
heartheld to where the mudbrick huts
their weathered windows daubed with useless crosses
their shattered doors   begin the slow descent
to earth   my earlier self turns in
darkening air   softly goes down with them
The boy only worms alive in his eyes
his face turned to the caves

---

*When we returned to the house we were a little crazy, as if it had been a nightmare.
My father marched ahead swiftly saying that he had much to do for his people; that
he must go from village to village to tell them what had happened ... A little later so
did my mother in her turn ... My brother left too ... and my little sisters.*

If in this poem you scream who will hear you
though you say *no one should cry out in vain*
your face dark mined with rage
Now in this strange mountain place
stripped by knowledge
I wait for you
Someone drunk stumbles the night path
snatching at a song or someone not drunk
I am so porous with fear
even the rustle of ants in the grass flows through me
but you are set apart
The catechists say *in heaven there is no male*
no female   that is a far foolishness
why else seeing you smelling of danger
and death do I want you so
your mouth   your clear opening in me

We began to build camps in the mountains where we would spend the night to pre-
vent the troops from killing us while we slept. In the daytime we had taught the chil-
dren to keep watch over the road ... We knew that the guerillas were up there in the
distant mountains. At times they would come down in order to look for food, in the
beginning we didn't trust them, but then we understood that they, at least, had weapons
to fight the army with.

You will not stop what you have begun
though I asked in the way a woman can
Since you have broken thus into life
soon someone will make a pattern
of your bones   of your skull
as they have with others
and what will fly out
what will escape from you torn apart
the boy and I must carry
In your sleep I went to the cenote*
in the moonlight I filled my shawl with flowers
threw them to the dark water
the ancient words fluting in my head
your son pinched awake to know what must come

My mother was captured (some) months later ... when all she could wish for was to die ... they revived her, and when she had recovered her strength they began torturing her again ... they placed her in an open field ... filled her body with worms ... she struggled a long time then died under the sun ... The soldiers stayed until the buzzards and dogs had eaten her. Thus they hoped to terrorize us. She doesn't have a grave. We, her children, had to find another way of fighting.

*cenote: a well occasionally used in ritual sacrifice (precolumbian)

Oh love this is silence   this is the full
silence of completion   we have swum through
terror that seared us to bone
rage lifted a cold hand to save us
so we became this surreal country
We have been bullet-laden air   fields that sprout
skulls   night that screeches and hammers
we have been hunger   whip   wind that sobs
feast days and drunken laughter
a rare kindness and pleasure
We have come through to the other side
here everything is silence   our quiet breathing
in this empty hut   our clay jugs full of light
and water   we are our corn our salt
this quiet is the strength we didn't know we had
our humanity no longer alarms us
we have found who we are
my husband our silence is the silence of blue steel thrumming
and of love
Our deaths shall be clear

---

*Our only way of commemorating the spilled blood of our parents was to go on fight-
ing and following the path they had followed. I joined the organization of the
Revolutionary Christians. I know perfectly well that in this fight one runs the great-
est risk ... We have been suffering such a long time and waiting.*

Your death is drenched in such light
that small things   the sky   branches
brushing against the cave mouth   the boy
stirring   make my skin crackle against damp blankets
As one gathers bullets carelessly spilled I gather your screams
all night I remember you   utterly lovely
the way you danced the wedding dance
rising dust clouding your sandals
your slow dark smile
You return to the predawn   leaving us
what remains when the flames die out of words
(small hard assertions
our beginnings
shards of the world you shattered
and ourselves)

Their death gave us hope, because it is not just that the blood of all those people be erased forever. It is our duty on this earth to revive it ... I fight so they will recognise me ... If I have taken advantage of this chance to tell the story of my life it is because I know that my people cannot tell their own stories. But they are no different from mine.

This testimony was collected by Elizabeth Burgos-Debray. Translated into Spanish by Sylvia Roubaud. This translation taken from the Mexican publication *Unomasuno*. It was published by *American Poetry Review* January/February 1983.

BLACK SISYPHUS

To propitiate the dreaming god at his centre
for months my father drove down green uneven

roads to the capital where tar flowed under
noonday heat in daily manoeuvres around new obstacles

to take form again in cold pale morning
he drove those roads in mutters searching through

the crumpled pathways of his brain while his
voice rose and stumbled in the sibilant argument

he enjoyed with life   he could not be
convinced that being human was not enough

that there was no bridge he could cross
he would not "forget de man" nor "leave

him to God"   these were his sky/trees/
his streets to name   was he not greeted

by all he passed   naming   from a wilderness
of loss his fathers created this island garden

he would not be cast out again   he
rode his right to words   pointed and named

the road from one way of life to another is hard
those who are ahead have a long way to go *

missionary zeal could not stomach such clarity
they damned him   thundered fire   brimstone   the sin

of pride   thus my father and his letters
raced weekly to the centre   the apology

won   he stood   nodded   bowed   strode in his own
echoing silence   out of lowered eyes/bells/incense

the worn organ's cough   out of village voices
wheeling in cracked Kyries

to stand on the church steps muttering:
it is enough to be a man today

his fingers kneading my six year old hands
as if they would refashion them

---

*Transtromer, "From an African Diary" (1963)

FRAMED

She is in your painting   the one you bought when the taxi
snarled in market lines   you jumped out and grabbed
a picture of stilted wooden houses against the vivid island
even then there was recognition

She is the woman in a broken pair of men's shoes   her
flesh slipped down like old socks around her ankles   a tray
of laundry on her head   I am there too   but I would not
be like her   at supper she set the one plate and the whole
cup at my place   for herself a mug a bowl my leavings
they said I resembled her   I spent hours before the mirror
training my mouth to different lines

At night while I read   she folded the blanket on her
narrow board   coalfire smooth on her face   she boiled
scrubbed   ironed   musk of soap and others soil like
mist around her head   often she dreamed   I would have
a maid   like her   she laughed   I studied harder harder
she grieved   I was grown a woman   I was grown
without affinity

For the calling   her eroded hands   cupped like a chalice
she offered me the blasted world as if to say   this is our
sacrament   drink   I would not   this is all there is   I
could not   I left school   I left   she faded
the island faded   styles changed   you hid the dusty
painting in the attic   But I am still there   the one in
middle ground   my face bruising lines of soft white
sheets   my hand raised as if to push against the frame

BIBLIOGRAPHY

Fables from the Women's Quarters. Stratford: Williams-Wallace, 1984.

Translation Into Fiction. Fredericton: Goose Lane Editions, 1984.

Travelling to Find a Remedy. Fredericton: Goose Lane Editions, 1986.

The Conception of Winter. Stratford: Williams-Wallace, 1989.

Under Black Light. Stratford: Williams-Wallace, forthcoming 1993.

Birth of an Angel. Fredericton: Goose Lane Editions, forthcoming 1992.

ANTHOLOGIES

Penguin's Book of Caribbean Verse. 1986.

Displaced Persons. Denmark/Australia: Dangaroo Press, 1988.

Nemiroff, Greta, editor. *Celebrating Women: Poetry and Short Stories by and about Canadian Women*. Toronto: Fitzhenry and Whiteside, 1989.

Sullivan, Rosemary, editor. *Poetry by Canadian Women*. Toronto: Oxford, 1989.

Scheier, Libby, Sheard, Sarah, & Wachtel, Eleanor, editors. *Language in Her Eye: Writing and Gender*. Toronto: Coach House Press, 1990.

Kanada. Germany: Konigshausen & Neumann, 1991.

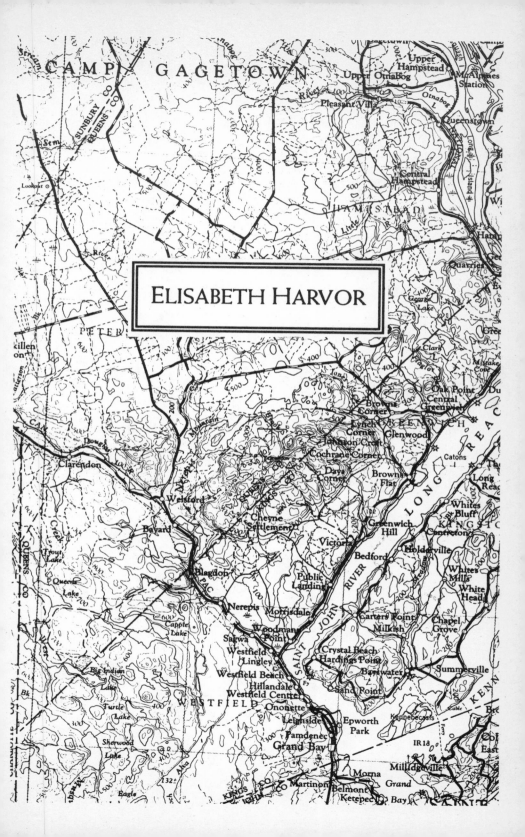

— Kim Chan

DOWN HERE, DOWN THERE

A THING I COULD NEVER HAVE UNDERSTOOD when I was a child: my parents had dangerous friends. They were acquainted with a Mr. and Mrs. Weasel whose shoestore was equipped with a foot X-ray machine, and my brother and sister and I would fight over whose turn it was to stand longest in that pulpit with a periscope mounted in it and gaze down at our toe-bones as they were so scientifically held in their ocean-green rectangles of quasi-medical light. But their best friend was a doctor who was the superintendent of one of the last TB sanatoriums on the Maritime coast. Because of friendship this doctor became our family doctor and once a year he would stretch my brother and me out on a clinical table and X-ray us. When I think of how powerful those old X-ray machines were I feel afraid, and when I add to their X-rays all the X-rays from the foot X-ray machine, I half-long, half-fear to gauge my older-sister bossiness, as if I could somehow determine, from this older and wiser distance, exactly how long I once (and more than once, in fact many times) gazed down at my toes in dangerous wonder.

More X-rays followed after a bout with pneumonia when I was living with the doctor and his family for two years while I attended high school in Saint John. And even more X-rays a few years later when I was a student nurse at a hospital on the other side of the city; all student nurses were routinely X-rayed every September — we were also the ones who would be asked by the lab techs to stay with the patients and hold them for difficult shots. Would we have dared to say no — in the days before people near the site of an X-ray were fitted out with lead aprons? It would never have occurred to us, in those innocent times.

I've heard that that hospital is no longer in use, and that the TB hospital where my parents' doctor-friend presided, in the eastern end of the city was, after antibiotics cleared the sanatorium of all of its patients, converted to a chronic care hospital. In fact the doctor slowly, horribly died there, of Alzheimer's Disease and other complications of old age, in the wards where he had once reigned as medical king — an irony that seems to me to be too terrible for either fiction or poetry. (But one I may nevertheless make use of, at some future date.)

As for what the orderly said to me on that long-ago afternoon, it became part of the poem "In the Hospital Garden." It's a poem in which I have tried to pit a baby who seems to be a radiation mutation against young girls who are being exposed to radiation in their work as nurses. This baby really existed, its father really was a radiologist on the staff of the hospital where I trained, and it really was transferred to the Contagious Diseases Annex where its assignment was to die quietly, secretly without fanfare or attention. Its chart contained a chilling directive: NO SUNSHINE, NO VITAMINS, NO SPECIAL CARE. Or possibly it was only NO VITAMINS, NO SPECIAL CARE, and it is only memory that adds sunshine, since sunshine could stand for so much that this baby tragically lacked. But the pavilion called the Fowler Pavilion was an invention. I wanted the name Fowler in the poem and I didn't know why, I *thought* it was because it was an old east coast family name, but I also must have wanted it because it could be seen as an explosion of the word "flower." Or at least, in retrospect, I believe that my unconscious wanted this; to scramble that word, to "mutate" it, to show some of the ways we have managed to foul (Fouler) our earthly nest.

The dangers of radiation are embodied by (again) the radiologist's mutated baby in a story called "Monster Baby." I have often used the same material in the two different forms and expect to do it often again. I don't see myself as only a fiction writer or only a poet. Some of my poems seem to me to work better than some of my stories, and some of my stories work better than some of my poems. I don't feel a whole lot of guilt when I steal from myself, either — if events or even echoes of the same imagery put in an appearance in different productions. In a part of a novel I've been working on recently, I used material I had earlier used in a poem called "The Street Where We Lived." And the beginning of a poem called "Living with Poets"

> Your skin is as soft as a
> wiener that hasn't been cooked yet,
> my youngest boy tells me
> as he inhales the length
> of my forearm

also appears in a somewhat different form, in this same novel, but in this case I may soon have to decide in which form it works best. Sometimes I'll write something in a notebook—a description of a woman, say, remembering a nightgown she owned when her children were babies and she'll be recalling its band of pink and grey smocking and the way "pablum used to get hardened in some of the smocked parts," and I won't know whether that'll work best in a poem or a story.

I loved having children, I loved that whole world — a world that seemed to heave with the physical. I felt — as I imagine so many women must feel — so trusted and useful. I could make a list of all the ways women with small children feel indispensable, but we all know all the ways and in any case I could never make a list that could hold a candle to some of the lists my children made when they were little. Lists about everything. In fact I used (or stole) a list from one of my young sons to end the story "Countries" (written in the late Sixties), a list that is made up of words that are the child's shorthand for naming the world, words that are shoved-together comic collections of consonants, printed by a child of three so hungry to learn to read and write that he (as so many small children do) invented his own vocabulary:

Crowne
Srench
Bloor
Bungo
Mator
Rpray
Neater
Zem
Eno
Brebut
Bibo
Plat
Ruzy
Drub
Zime

And when I described the child's way of seeing the world that the mother in another of the early stories learns to make use of, I wanted to catch all the ways in which parents see children as both limitation and revelation. The story is this: a little boy has been sick, there's been a great snowstorm, and after it's over and he is better, his mother zips him into his navy-blue nylon snow-suit, "the one that gives him the high wasp waist" and takes him for a walk out into the new world. The mother has a headache and wants above all things *not to be disturbed*, and so she thinks:

> There is something about being with little children at times
> when you so much don't want to be with them, that jacks your
> perceptions up, that cracks open your old way of thinking ... .
> you have to be starved for sleep, and you have to wish very
> much to be alone. It also helps if you've just nursed the child
> and he's been cranky, and if, during the last twenty-four hours,
> you've sometimes hated him, preferably intensely. If you are
> entirely by yourself, you are sometimes disoriented by the
> newness, the strangeness, the significance of it, but when you are
> with a child, you are fiercely fighting for the right to think your
> own thoughts; and then you do think them, and you think them
> fast, wholesale, entire, against the absolute certainty that you will
> be interrupted again and again. Sometimes it's a good way to
> have to think ... .

❖

I've always been hooked on body-processes. Especially women's. In one of the first stories I wrote, in the early Sixties, I wrote about menstruation and the menopause. The story is called "The Hudson River"; "The Hudson River" is what a character in it named Mrs. Hudson calls her menstrual flow. And breastfeeding, Maternity Wards, breast cancer and excess body hair are central elements in several of the other early stories. So it wasn't a great jump for me to go more deeply into breastfeeding in "Madam Abundance." Or to write what I could never have conceived of writing when I was younger, a kind of nostalgic lament for menstruation (in the poem "Bloom, Rain"), or to write about women and their vulvas in the poem "Down There."

In fact while I was working on the ending of "Down There," I realized that the poem could work in a double way, that the *down there* could refer not only to the vulva (from the woman's-eye view) but also to the world (from the God's-eye view) and that the words with which the poem ends ("Can you make wind? Can you make water?") could be more than a send-up of genteel hospital euphemisms for urine and gas, they could also be taken quite literally to be Bible-style questions that a person, given the opportunity, really might want to ask God.

And in the novel I'm working on now, there's a scene where a young wife wakes up in the night with her breasts "hard as footballs, sore" and because she is weaning her baby and so doesn't want to wake him up for a feeding, she makes a night search for her breast pump. But she can't find it in its usual drawer, down among the Tahitian flowered half-slips and the flimsy summer panties, and so she wanders through the dark house looking for it in unlikely (and therefore likely) places — the bathtub, her baby's playpen. She's sure she'll sight it any minute, standing sentinel over a child's city of blocks, its white rubber bulb end transforming it into a tiny water tower. But no. Finally she gives up and uncurls her husband's sleeping hand and kisses it, then asks him if he can suck her nipples a little, to take the pressure off. He tries, but the milk is too sweet for him to swallow. (And it *is* very sweet, human milk, as any woman who's ever squeezed a few drops of it on the inside of her wrist and then licked them up will tell you; I recall that it tasted as natively rich as goat's milk but as if someone had warmed it up and dropped a medicine dropperful of honey down into it.) And so the husband goes down to the kitchen to get a teacup to spit his wife's milk into, and while she's waiting for his return, she goes over to the window to watch the snow falling — new snow falling on old snow — and as she releases the hardest breast, wintry sparks of air ignite it, making the whole breast electric.

I like the playfulness that seems more natural to poetry that it ever does to fiction. With this proviso: that it open the door to some deeper emotion. Take the long poem "Afterbirth": this is probably the most free-wheeling poem I'll ever write, but every artistic dilemma I encountered in writing it either masked (or *was*) an ethical dilemma. The poem has a cat and a mouse in it (a dead mouse; in fact, two dead mice), but it is also a poem which plays cat and mouse with ideas about memory — particularly sexual and disturbing (or at least puzzling) memories from childhood. But what was most disturbing to me as the poem evolved were not the memories themselves — I was used to them, after all, since they were my own — but my moral position as raconteur, *vis à vis* the memories. I was intrigued by the tension between the wish to examine and the wish to refuse the clandestine seductions of dislocated and isolated memories, and I was probably eager to pit *those* memories against the empirical evidence of a long and trusting association between a father and a daughter as a way of exploring both the thrill and the burden of being adored. (Adored and adoring.) But I never set out to do this; I never set out to do anything; if I did, I don't think I could write. And yet the images make curious counterarguments so that certain renegade memories crouch in the unconscious like stowaways whose dialect I can't quite understand. As the narrator (who both wants and does not want to stay in the dark) says at one point, "Memories, if I can just figure them out, might point the way to this childhood, that childhood ... ." But she also says, seeming to argue for more dissembling, not more clarity, or maybe only arguing for the complexity of things as they are, "but can't any image leapfrog over itself to more and more meanings?"

In real life there are transformations that are dangerous (Mr. and Mrs. Weasel's once-modern but now dated and malevolent machine), and there are transformations that are entertaining. An example: Mr. and Mrs. Weasel's son Larry changed his name to Lawrence Earl when he grew up to become a writer of adventure novels set in exotic places. And why not? If a frog can turn into a prince, why can't a weasel turn into an earl? But the questions I have about transformations when I'm writing are questions about the morality of certain transformations of art. These are some of the hard questions. Still, all the doubts, anguish, guilts, euphoria, second thoughts and wishes for revision pale — for me, anyway — beside the two great questions, questions that seem to have less to do with being a writer than they have to do with being human. And the one question seeming illogically to follow the other (although to me it seems to follow it *logically*):

Why is the world so imperfect?

And why must we leave it?

❖

BIOGRAPHICAL NOTE

Elisabeth Harvor writes both poetry and fiction. Her story collections are If Only We Could Drive Like This Forever, *and a re-release of her first book,* Women and Children, *under the title* Our Lady of All the Distances. *Her first collection of poetry,* Fortress of Chairs, *is forthcoming from Véhicule Press in 1992. She works as a sessional lecturer in the Department of English at York University, Toronto. Her work has appeared in Arc, Event, The Hudson Review, The Malahat Review, The New Yorker, Ontario Review, Fiddlehead, The Antigonish Review, Poetry Canada Review, Prairie Fire, Prism International, and many other periodicals. She was one of the winners of The Malahat Long Poem Prize in 1990, and was the first-prize winner of the League of Canadian Poets' National Poetry Prize in 1991.*

DOWN THERE

The water in the hot water tank
had to be saved for the dishes, washing
floors, and so on fall and winter mornings and on
spring mornings, too — the peeping
lilac bobbing at the cramped bathroom window —
my mother and sister and I would take turns
squatting in the cold-hollow tub to
pour a tin jug of warm water over ourselves
down there. Rural hygiene! Only in July and August
would we be free of the jug
with a quick dip from the dock. Some
hot and windy mornings we were even too
sleep-stunned to swim and would only stand,

up to our throats in the water,
our fists on our puckered, elasticized hips,
our legs in the military At Ease position,
a sexual way for a young girl to stand in a river,
feeling the water
offering its play of
thrilled, rippled coldness.

Years later,
I was taught, in the purposeful, deadly bright light
of a hospital morning, the sleight-of-hand of
lifting drugged hips onto warm bedpans, the
clinical magic of pouring a tin pitcher of
warm water — this time marked with the

formal braille of measurement — over post-operative
women patients *down there*, the trick being to

trick the body
into thinking it was already doing
what it must do.

I did not recall then, as I recall now,
those girlhood ablutions.

You need time for that, that kind of linkage,
memory begetting memory
as water begat water.

But oh, those hospital questions!
So like the questions a
child might ask of God or a parent:

Can you make wind?
Can you make water?

THE SKY OR THE FOREST OR THE CUPBOARD

After lunch one of the visitors
offers to read the Tarot for us, "Oh!"
cries our mother. "Oh, I don't know ... "
Odd — she is the parent I feel afraid of,
yet she is the one who believes childhood
should be kept sweet always — nothing

frightening. This must be my fault.
One rainy evening when an older cousin
was left to look after us and was browsing
among the books in the basement to
hunt down the story of some shawled waif or

good girl, and, wobbly-thighed in her tan shorts that
had a stain near the cuff — we wondered,
Is it blood? — read to us of the voice
crying out of the sky or the forest or the cupboard,
*If your poor dear mother could see you now, her poor
heart would break with grief,* I wept

so bitterly that our parents, when later they
were told of it, banished the brothers Grimm
and Hans Christian Andersen (whistling Hans,
dancing Hans, Hans from the movie) to the glass-faced
cabinet in the upstairs hallway. After this
(and after our baths; this was on windy evenings,

only one star in the sky) our parents would take
turns reading to us about the exploits
of a family of pigs who were also inventors,
or the domestic arrangements of Rat and Toad
in *The Wind in the Willows*. But this was when
we were babies. Now we're old enough to make ourselves

go stiff and glassy-eyed, now we cannot be pried
from the long table as, with destiny's
snap, each card is laid down. Right away we can see
that the cards' pictures have been stolen
out of the banned books of our childhood:
a hefty boy driving a stick

into a field of sticks; a hand coming out
of a cloud to offer a chalice to a sad man
sitting under a tree; a queen seated on a throne
in an orchard. (And everyone lost, lost in somebody's
tender or evil dream of golden ripeness.) But wait,
the Hanged Man is only a Hanged Boy, really,

cheerful and Nordic, hung
upside down by an ankle and ordered
to do calesthenics. Between the naked
lovers, above the purple mountain,
it is the blue skies
that are terrible.

IN THE HOSPITAL GARDEN

We couldn't love the radiologist's baby,
We were too afraid of her to love her,
      too afraid
She would die one night in our arms.
Down in the Contagious Diseases Annex (it was where
She'd been sent to die, out of the world's way)
We would pick her up to feed her
Her midnight bottle of milk. But she would
      seem
Every moment, to be in danger of choking:
Her brain deformed — not there, almost,

Her breaths plunged and wild,
Hooked to some
      fearful kite
Of wrong ideas about breathing:
It was with hit-and-miss gasps she would try
To swallow. The staff in Maternity had sent down
A white shoebox, a mound of her tiny clothes
      puffed up in it —
Two exquisitely smocked flowered
Nightgowns and a miniature flannelette
Bolero jacket with a pink silk
      featherstitch trim.

It was hard, feeding her, not to think
Of her father, striding the hallways with what
Looked like a black fountain pen
      clipped

To the breast pocket of his lab coat — but we all
Knew what it really was: a Geiger counter, only
            pretending
To be a fountain pen! — and harder still
Not to think of her mother, whose room we had invented
At least five reasons to walk by
            on the morning following
The infamous birth. We passed by trollies
            bearing
Rows of stone-heavy green teapots and aluminum basins
Of eggs so warm they might just a moment before have been
            collected from some giant hen
In the hospital garden. And then we saw her.
But she looked exactly as we would have expected
A doctor's wife to look — had brought that
            air of clandestine glamour
Into the palace of birth and death with her,
Was a slender combed blond, her nightgown
            a long gauzy white shift
With shoestring straps, expensively simple, not
            defaced by
Eyelet or lace. Flanked like a casket

By flowers, she was sitting
Cranked up in her bed in the randomly
            snowing grey morning light
Unhappily smoking and reading. I thought of menstrual
Cramps whenever I walked by her room, for she was constantly
Drawing up a leg and straightening it, then drawing up
            the other leg
And straightening it. When her baby
Finally died the following August (rumour had it
That the radiologist had never allowed her

To see it, dead or alive)

The news ran through the nurses' residence,
              solemn wildfire —
Dead, people said, Dead at last. We were still
Only students but not too young to
Say it was a blessing, and later that
              fogged monday,
Sitting up in the third floor kitchen and
Drinking bad coffee till midnight
              we spoke of it
Again. A tall girl with her navy cape
              hugged to her over her pyjamas
Remembered one of the orderlies
On Female Surgery, the way he used to go around telling
The students they didn't have to agree to
Stay with the patients
While they were being X-rayed. I knew this boy,
He'd said the same thing to me
              one sunlit afternoon
When he'd overheard a brisk girl from X-ray tell me
To "Stay with the patient, please, and hold her."
I thought of him as I took
              little sips
Of my destroyed-tasting coffee, I remembered the way
He'd handcuffed the upper part of my arm, the way he'd
              spoken
With such a stern sweetness ("You don't have to do it"),
              like he was a boy who loved me
And was telling me I wasn't obliged
              to go to bed with
One of his rivals. I remembered how we'd
Stood together in the fourth floor

Utility Room of the Fowler Pavilion, how the window there
        looked down
On the walking buoys of white blossoms being nodded

On the uneven seas of the hospital's
        lilac hedges
As if there were little steps the turreted flowers
Had to sleepily walk up and down, little steps
        up and down
In that drowsy leafy ocean. (Some of us
Are dead now — three of the students drinking coffee in that
        fogbound
Jam-smelling kitchen were dead by our fifteenth
Reunion. Their disease was the disease
        hospital decorum
Had taught us to call by its first two letters:
CA of the cervix, CA of the breast.) But now someone
        was speaking
Of the baby again, was calling it "a radiation mutation."
There was a silence then, but
        what I feel now
Looking back — oh, years later! — is a tender shame
For what I feel certain we all secretly,
With a deadly thrill thinking:

        We are here
        This is now

        There will never
        Be a time
        More modern
        Than now is

MADAM ABUNDANCE

A pen and ink drawing might begin
with the head, the shoulders, but this
one could begin with a circle
and in that circle the lopsided
eye of the drowsed nipple or,
when it's aroused or in use,
that stubbed pink castle of flesh in its pebbled
moat of pigment, sturdy schoolboy's eraser,
sucked and gleaming and
hung in the milk-heavy
bag of the breast.

The baby, bee to flower,
blindly nosing its way to its
medicine dropper of milk, and for the mother

the sting of the mouth of her
firstborn bee

Attachments!
The string of drool connecting the
tiny white pill of the miniature cardigan's
single button to one of the six
much more pearly and womanly buttons

on the milk-dampened blouse of the breast,
this drooled string the sibling to a

drooped string of garden saliva
slung between flower and flower
(the taller, the smaller)
on a Monday that will be
a hot, humid Monday
morning in August. But now

it's fogged sunrise,
hour of non sequitur:
memories of husband-breath
the night this baby may have been
begun — the husband bashful and

bowing in at the door
of the parlour with his
come-out-to-the-garden-to-play
smile. He is young, he is scrubbed but
erotic, his mouth cool as
ether but with mint in it,

the wife is lolled on the sofa
reading *War and Peace*, she is risen warm
as baked bread, she is half-brown
from the sun and her blouse three-quarters
undone, a drift of rose-petal pink, her eyes
demurely sly, their lids

such drooped and wanton
know-it-all flowers that when the husband
drops to one knee to take a nipple
into his mouth, his own eyes
closed with the pleasure and gallantry of it, his

fingers making their male slide up the tulip-cleft
in one of the shoved-up legs
of her shorts, she twists to and from him until
he is forced to kiss and tickle her up,
to lead her to bed,

to lead her to this: she is
wearing a maternity smock over the
puckered shorts tied with the drawstring,
she is barefoot, she is ironing one of the
husband's shirts, the iron nosing its way to a

stitched armpit, steaming and hooting
its way into the wrinkled cove of a pocket. And how
does it smell? Oh, sweet! Sweeter than anything!
Like those pouches on lupin flowers that smell
like pepper, like laundry
you've just pulled down off the line — the peppery
smell of wildflowers along with the
salt of laundered
perspiration coming up

with the steam. But now it's a year later,
now the baby has come out into the world,
now it's time for the wife to tuck her
fed bee into his cradle, but first she must
carry him to the window to say hello to the fogged
sunrise, to hear the rusted cry of the big birds
of dawn (too tropical by half for the
concrete spires and towers of Toronto), to be
jogged to the view of the whole city sleeping,
the upstairs screened-in back sunporches

still all sagged and lost
in their hives of leaves
and sleep

Sometimes she feels scared and humble
thinking of the future, thinking
What if. What if something should happen
to her baby! What if she should fail him!
What if she's marked to become another statistic (highway, divorce),

what if the husband should become
the dear departed? Should depart
into the afterlife? Not the afterlife of
the Victorian husband — black crepe and sorrow —
but being a modern man in a windbreaker and carrying
his flight bag out to his car,

merely and terribly
into the afterlife of another life?
Someday — impossible to believe — all this
will be far behind her, this baby

lying in the incubated smell of
his own proud warm urine, his tiny hands'
delicate ownership of her breast,
the way he must see her, the welcoming

tumbled leer of the nipple.
But this morning she feels no pity
for that older woman (herself, turned old,
old as her own mother), this morning she feels
only her own power (youth, cruelty), here

in this kitchen, holding this
sweet boy in her sun-warmed arms,

this morning she is Madam Abundance,
nothing can touch her

AT THE HORSE PAVILION

We lost you once, at the Horse Pavilion,
on a day of snappy wind
beating five flags above that brilliant

nightmare green in the sun and beyond
prayer but ready to live on a diet of it
for the rest of our days, we ducked and

ran among faces made blank or tender by our
terror, so that we understood for the first time
that this was the was way the world was truly divided:

into those faces that could be startled into
goodness, and those that could not, but none of
them worth anything at all to us except for what

they could tell us as we kept calling out to them
the only words left to us, *A little boy!*, and the
colours of the clothes you were wearing, while the

polished horses kept mindlessly
clearing gates that were hardships, but distant,
whitewashed, the hardships of others, and sounds

mocked us too, in that whinnied bright air — a
ring of faint surf, the civil, evil sound of
horsemen's applause, and we ran into each other and

ran back and ran through the stadium of stalls and

sick straw-smell and ran out into the sun of the
Pavilion's mud plaza and there you were, on

the other side of the soot track that lead toward
the weeping green park, your eyes fixed without
flinching on the main doorway, waiting for us

to come out sometime before
dark and we fled to you, crying
your name and I could see in your eyes how hard

you'd been standing your ground against terror,
how long you'd been forbidding yourself to
invent us, as if in inventing us you'd have

lost all chance to see us come out to you, but
how brilliant you seemed, having saved yourself
from harm, you didn't know it, you turned your

face to the taut thigh of skirt, not to cry, and
we walked that way, my hand
holding your head to me while I could have

sworn I could feel you inhaling what I was thinking
through the skirt's grass-engraved cotton:
Until this moment I never knew what love is.

SATURDAY AFTERNOON AT THE CLINIC

The only patient,
I study the reproductions — Monet
at Antibes: the blown
spring-to-the-hilt
havoc of it,

all wreckage and blossoms.
Also one of Van Gogh's bedrooms —
the one at Arles, maybe,
making me think of another bedroom

dog's-hair, splintered
blue-green of the child-like wooden bed

the picture's basin and jug
chopped out of blue paint

Ordered alternative
to Monet's reckless springtime,
framed,

windblown
taunt behind glass

Plunged light
with its message:

This is the world!
The world you should have chosen!

Not these public armchairs
in robin's-egg vinyl

Not this
clinic among leaves

*

Purse hugged up into high clasp
between armpit and heart,
I look until I can't look
any longer, then out of apprehension
pretending to be boredom
set myself an assignment: Compose ten phrases
making use of the word *only*

To begin: My husband, long ago,
posed stiffly beside me while a
burly man in a smock
embroidered with a bunioned
black cross made out of x's
is speaking of "this woman,"
asking him to vow to cleave
only unto her

Next — but this is
years later — a clear male voice singing
a song beginning *Only the lonely* ... making
an arch of pure sound high over his own life

After this, someone saying about
someone: *Only three months to live.* Then
there are all those moments of misplaced
trust in Fate, someone speaking of someone who
only ran out to the corner store for a minute
to get some nutmeg and cleanser
but then:

the bomb fell,
the gas main exploded,
the house burst into flame, it
only took half an hour
to burn all the way
down to the ground

Only the children were home at the time,
they had been told to
only play quietly, to

not light the candles,
the littlest girl
only wanted to see what
her sister's braids would look like

burning

(she was only four)

Only tell me this:
what wrong turning
did I take in my life
that I should find myself

indoors
on a day such as this one?

The grass the healthy green
of the grass in the graveyard?

The strong
sun burning down?

Somewhere out in the world
cold lakes
are throttling

the plunged sound
of men's laughter

hot summer winds
are bathing
some women's skin

BLOOM, RAIN

How do we do it?
Learn how to be old?
When it's not
what we planned on? Once
I walked down the street
with only one thought
in my head (your name), it was
raining, there were tipped shelves
of boxes, they smelled of wet wood
and bananas and the bananas were
wet and the green grapes
were wet, I was having my period
(I was always having my period
when it was raining) and

everywhere there were umbrellas
raised up, ruby shelters
lit by rainy-sky light
and the mounds of the garden too, petal-littered,
everything driven,
rained down
onto the shrapnel,
the sharp stones of the

pocked lawns and gravel and
under the small hoisted world
of every umbrella, people hurrying
or plotting (people plot more when
it's raining, a little-known fact

from the annals of rain-lore — they
plan for sunlight, they plan
to be happy) and this
petal carnage, this windy
damp, these umbrellas
all had something to do with seepage, with
pelvic pain — with pelvic pain in
the rain and me walking along and
thinking your name and taking
such comfort in that persistent
dulled pain. Now, years later,
people walk in the rain as if they
are vowing things; to listen to more of
the kind of music that stirs
the soul, for instance — the kind of music
that makes you remember
you haven't lived the life

you wanted to live — no,
I don't imagine them vowing this,
I'm too unhappy to imagine other
people vowing things, I
won't give them the credit, I'm locked
in the egomania of regretting my life,

but oh, think of it! Never again to feel
that dragged young ache in the womb,
never again to feel that easing warm bloom
of the flood from your body

bathing me in every part of my body — the way
it tore a cry from me
and long before this, even — we are dancing,

your hand, fingers splayed on the small of my back and
formally steering me, heat blooming in
your palm, heat breathing in and out
of the heart of your stilled hand,

beyond us a line of
hung shirts and sweaters
wet with the colours of fog, of goldenrod,

turning as we turn,
the day's foggy too — it's almost dark,

now it *is* dark ... is it
raining?
Memory wants rain

the night wind
in the shot garden —

a rattling,
an unfurling,

the black windows,
rain

BIBLIOGRAPHY

Women and Children. Ottawa: Oberon, 1973.

If Only We Could Drive Like This Forever. Markham: Penguin, 1988.

Our Lady of All the Distances. (Reprint, revised, of *Women and Children*) Toronto: HarperCollins, 1991.

Fortress of Chairs. Montreal: Signal Editions, Véhicule Press, forthcoming, 1992.

ANTHOLOGIES (SELECTED)

Modern Canadian Stories. Toronto: Bantam, 1976.

The Penguin Book of Modern Canadian Short Stories. Markham: Penguin, 1982.

Sullivan, Rosemary, editor. *More Stories by Canadian Women*. Toronto: Oxford University Press, 1987.

Ondaatje, Michael, editor. *From Ink Lake*. Toronto: Lester, Orpen Dennys, 1990.

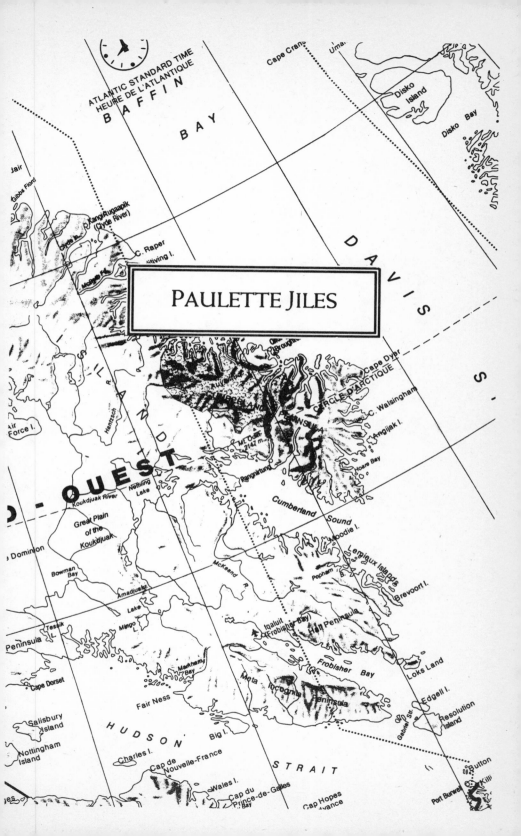

PAULETTE JILES

—Jim Johnson

YOU THERE

The LONGEST POEM IN THIS SECTION, "Song to the Rising Sun," was written for radio. It was written to be heard. When I was working as a journalist in both print and radio, I had to learn the difference between the written and the spoken word and master the skills of both. There is a world of difference. I am much happier working with things that are meant to be heard. I was lucky to get the assignment to do a long radio poem. I learned a great deal during the composition of it. I had already read and pondered Lords' work on the compositional techniques of the Greek epic poems, as found in the first half of this century in Yugoslavian folk epics. I had a good background in storytelling from my own family; not only storytelling but "Dirty Dozen" rhyming, singing and clever can-you-top-this catch-phrasing. And not least, the power of the phrasing of the King James Bible as recited aloud and expounded on to a knowledgeable and critical audience. Let's hear it for Isaiah. Like the Yugoslavian folk singers, those old people and those community churches are dying away, slipping away into electronic noise and the seven-second imperative, but I remember them. This century is the first century in our history in which one can hear poetry and not be in the presence of the speaker. We can sit alone without others, without being part of a body called "audience" and receive or consume poetry, drama and song without having to give anything back to a living presence. There is no eye contact, no release and pause as a chorus or choir comes on with massed voices to free us from the intensity of the single performer or the monologue. There are no shifts and no changes for the isolated listener, and the environment is also under the listeners' control as well. No drafty halls, the crumpling crush of programs, fussy children or the wild desire to sneak out and smoke. You can remain isolated, untouched and pure. But I wanted to go back to these older devices that grew out of the contact between a performer and the audience in front of her because they are more suited to me and unpure and sometimes quite chaotic. I like them. Just because you or perhaps one or two others are sitting there unseen by me or by the actors is no reason not to use these techniques, as if we were indeed in a drafty hall with a bad mike, fussy children, people crushing programs, sneaking out for a smoke, etc.

I have always been interested in the radio audience. When I was putting together documentaries for CBC radio in the early Seventies, I would listen to the producers talk about things like the size and composition of different audiences for different shows. I would read letters written by listeners in far places. I would interview people over phone link-ups as far away as Beirut. It seemed to be an audience that was bigger than, but included, the reading audience for poetry. One always seemed to be more in the presence of the radio audience and I liked that. The audience appeared to be flexible, interested, alert, forgiving of small mistakes — an audience that responded with vitality. The feel of the presence of a non-hostile, non-judgemental audience can bring the best out of a writer or a performer.

"Song to the Rising Sun" uses very old devices; repetition of an initial phrase combining with variant tags, use of different sorts of sentences (interrogative, as well as declarative), those long series of driving imperatives, a fall-back into the softer, intimate "feelings" lyric, the direct address to the audience and doubled, chorused or massed voices. In university I used to hear professors expound on *The Odyssey*, and the techniques the poet used, and how very brilliant they were, and I could never figure out why poets weren't using them now. In university the entire current of contemporary poetry flowed straight into the private lyric of feeling; that and that only. That was the poetry I began to write; when I could find the time and the head-space, I wrote lyrics. But I was fascinated by the older techniques. So I used them.

A final consideration about poetry that is written to be heard is time. Poetry recited aloud happens in a certain amount of time that is controlled by the speaker. It asks for a suspension of will on the part of the audience. You can't put it down like a book and come back later, flip back and re-read a line, make notes in the margins or underline words. Your only choice is to get up and leave in the dark, stumble over people, "excuse me, excuse me, my cat just died ..." or whatever, and creep out the door with a bang and a flash of the hall light. The listener is asked to give over his/her control of time to the speaker, to abandon that solitary, individual control which each member of the audience would have over a book in the hand. And although an audience sitting out in the darkness can be very forgiving of some mistakes (as I well know), of others, like when a reader inadvertently bores them, or imposes on them, they are not. I don't know how important this issue of control is; perhaps we just wish to surrender as little control as possible in our lives. This discussion could go on forever. It's a different world. I hope I haven't bored you. I told the editors of this anthology that I nattered on too much about this subject but they insisted on something longer than three lines. So to bring this to an end, I will emphasize that writing poetry to be heard is entirely my own trip, I don't teach it or insist other people write it. It's just that with radio you get all these sound effects. I like noise. I like artful noise. So when you are reading "Song" you will have to fill in the soundscapes yourself, you there alone with the book.

❖

BIOGRAPHICAL NOTE

Paulette Jiles was reared in various small towns in the Missouri Ozarks and Missouri River counties. She has traveled extensively in North America, Europe and North Africa. After working as a freelance radio reporter for the CBC, Jiles worked for ten years in the Arctic and sub-Arctic for Native communication groups. She taught writing at David Thompson University in Nelson, BC. In 1984, "Celestial Navigation" scooped the Governor General's Award, the Pat Lowther Award and the Gerald Lampert Award — the only book ever to have won all three prizes. She subsequently won the National Magazine Award, the McClelland& Stewart Award, the Canadian Newspaper Award for Aerial Photography and the ACTRA Radio Award as Best Writer, Original Drama.

GOING TO CHURCH

This is Sunday morning, July 16, 1958, Cole Camp, Butler County, Missouri, population 100 and just look at all these people getting ready for church. We are only 150 miles from the Arkansas border down here, which seems to loom dangerously close. Whatever bad happens, happens to the south of us. There are too many layers of irrelevant dresses but it seems I and every other teenage girl down here have been hired to play extras in *Gone With the Wind*. There are hot irons and potentially torn nylons. The tar on county road double E helplessly melts in the furnace of July, decorated with squashed, imbedded salt-and-pepper king snakes.

In the hot, expanding morning I rise up over the necks of dresses like yeast dough, and precisely the same colour. Hooks and eyes and zippers, the garter belts and elastic waists of petticoats, everything needs repairing and stitching and hooking up.

The men dress in simple, decent clothes, my brother Elroy is absorbed in the mysteries of the Windsor knot. Their pants are held up by brown and honest belts which require no more than the brains of a two-year-old to fasten.

But I am educated, I have spent hours in the encyclopedia, I know that South American Indian men in *The World Book* are the ones who decorate themselves; they spend hours painting their faces and stick bird of paradise feathers through their noses. Did you hear what? Is she talking? Never mind, Poppa Daddy, she just said something about somebody having a bird of paradise feather up their nose.

I look at my ironed and lacy dress laid out on the bed and I really want to be neolithic and hulk around the village in primitive weaves with beads made out of rocks and zircons. No dice, not in this town. The high heels now after six months' wear have scraped off their heel caps, the forefoot bulges out, full of big and little toes, the points bend up like coffeepot spouts. Does God really want us to wear this crap? In the blue-hot morning the bells ring and ring.

Down the road the Pentecostals weep and howl and walk into walls, but only on special occasions. In our Baptist church, which is the established one of the region, there will be only moderate demands at the end of the sermon for sinners to come up and repent with everybody looking at you and thinking about your clothes and what you have done in them. Thoughts like lint in the pockets and linings.

Meanwhile we sweat and fan ourselves with pictures of Jesus, sing, twist around on the pews. The starched laces cut into my thighs until they look like basketweave and I hope nothing gives way. There is so much that *can* give way, therefore it will; the zipper of this too-tight bodice, the treacherous garter belt, the perilous elastics of petticoats. Only the big, serious girdle with its rubberized tube will hold out, despite everything, to the very end. They will bury me in the goddamned thing.

(Is there no other way to be? Out of this green and steaming town I suspect there are other modes of existence. A Cherokee woman appears out of history, displaced and immediate, walking through New Echota in the early morning. She is surrounded by several vital colours and the air is red with morning. In her basket are blue things, spirits, green corn, a white luna moth, animal pelts. But history shuts her down; they are moving up even now, animal crackers from Georgia in stolen uniforms.)

We walk to church. I am in the centre of innumerable systems, a complex machine. Is this what being a young lady means? No doubt. Feet are being bound, here comes the *chador*, the walls are closing in on the *harim*. All around me women are trying to elevate like floating ice creams despite the heat, and the iron lace, and the hooks. They are possessed with themselves and well they ought to be, the centre of complex and disintegrating systems constantly in repair. (Can man be saved? the preacher asks, which means I have to think this out by myself, single-handed.) (No.) Explore nothing. Develop a pleasing manner. Contemplate your tubes.

In the Sunday-school class for young adults we play riddle games. What is a woman's crowning glory, asks the teacher, who is the lady that operates the town switchboard. I think desperately of crown and head and then I say hair. No, ha ha, it is her son! Son-sun, get it? Elroy smirks from behind his Windsor knot. Somehow I know this doesn't work out. Is something wrong with my hair? What do I take this so seriously? All this hot Sunday I take seriously the dreadful, precarious system of female clothes and shoes, the green, sizzling Ozarks, the whiteframe church and its eloquent bells, the Jesus fans and the overhead fans. Thut, thut, thut, they have one word, maybe it is the word of surrender or praise, perhaps it is the slow chorus of a world of eternal Sunday; the madhouse.

Outside a line of hills runs by, throwing treats and leaves. Turnback Creek boils with springwater, the crawdads celebrate Sunday and escape several raccoons. A cave opens its mysterious interior for visitors. Corn patches reflect a team of suns and the cobs fuse. There is some maroon music being played, elegantly, with hautboys and a viola da gamba in the shade of the chinquapin trees. Sometimes we carry our souls in our fists, tightly, against those who would extract them from us, like a storekeeper gently extracting pennies from the fists of children at Loller's station where we used to stop on the way to church, to buy candy with our plate money; and we wanted the candy but we would not give up the pennies either;

and what you have to do is open your fist, and it will suddenly spring up like a luna moth; and then you are on the road to New Echota, which leads through mountain valleys, at the thirty-sixth parallel, and you will be transfixed by a fox looking at you out of the jewelweed, who has just darted out of your heart and into the world. It is no smaller nor any happier than any other fox, or any other heart-bearing ore, red as Iron Mountain, and he or she will disappear like an idea into the world of legends;

the thick shushing of fans reminds us we are in church, worshipful. What will it avail a woman if she gain her own mind but lose her soul? All right, I will lose my soul. Not once but a hundred times. As many times as it takes. Turn now to page 145 and sing are you washed in the blood. No.

ONE SISTER (for Sunny)

One sister will always be fat and the other one thin.
One sister will look good in yellow and the other one won't,
and the one who doesn't look good in yellow
won't be able to carry a tune, either.
Who took my yellow dress?
Who borrowed my blue shoes?
Susan Marie, you took my 100 percent real silk scarf
and you didn't even ask me if you could borrow it!
Amanda Jean got in my diary and read it and anybody who
reads somebody else's diary deserves
anything they get.

There will always be one sister who isn't good at math
and one who has wide feet.
The one who has wide feet will be the one who discovers
the drop of blood on the stairs
near the woodstove.
It will be she who knows
that, if you pour wine on it,
the drop of blood will speak
and name the murderer.

One sister will cover for the other one when
the wrong prince shows up, pimply and alcoholic,
with a glass slipper.

(But the story is all wrong! The one with the wide feet
is the one with the delicate skin —
she hid her sister in the laundry basket
because she was so thin.)

There will always be one sister who betrays
the other ones.
Ah, we know whose fault it is.
It's always somebody else's fault;
it's the one who is good at math,
she just can't find her path
in life, she has to work in this roadhouse
carrying trays of beer,
and the other sisters will tell you
she used to sleepwalk in the night
and was once found walking down the railroad tracks
carrying some matches for her daddy
who was a brakeman at that time
for the Burlington and Illinois.

One sister will get divorced and the other one
will stay married forever
and the third one will never get married at all
and will charge a lot of clothes to her account
at a big downtown store.
Dad will always have loved one best and hated one most
and then there was the baby of the family. The family.
The family.
One sister will get married and divorced and have a love
affair in fifteen minutes flat from a standing start
and yet the other one will take all day to
find her hairpins,
only to discover they're all in her hair.

One sister will, at some time in her life, yell
at the other ones:
"You ruined my life! All of you!
You made my childhood totally miserable!"

Then there is the sister who has no sisters
and, in fact, makes them up.
She invents for herself all of the above scenes.
For her, books will open like wicker trunks
full of things she already knew were there
but couldn't get at.
Until now.
It is a delicate cloth, and very old.

One sister will travel to foreign places and see
the Tower of London and the other will take a course
in Mary Kay Cosmetics and then lose all her receipts.
"I never had much luck," she says, from her porch
in Butler County, as she fans herself with a Jesus fan.
One sister will always have had to ride the mule while
the other will get to take Daddy's saddle horse.
The two of them go for the mail like this,
arguing fiercely all the way down Pike Creek Road
"Fair! Unfair! Fair! Unfair!"
Sisters argue like Philadelphia lawyers.

One sister will explain her life in terms of men,
what they have done to her, what they
haven't done to her,
what she wishes they would do to her
or with her, or without her,
and the other sister will listen angrily, tapping her fingers

on the tablecloth.
But they are trying so hard to get along,
so the one who is doing the little number on the tablecloth
gets up to make more coffee and thinks,
"She's still talking about men,"
and this kind of thing will always divide the sisters somehow.
Even though they don't know it.
Zinnias loom with accurate brown looks
out of the garden and their hairdos steam in
the hot sun.
One sister will just have come back from an assignment
in a strange place. There are stamps in weird scripts
all over her passport;
the other one sings in the choir, dazzled by notes.
Why is everybody getting divorced all of a sudden?
It must be something in the water, says the other sister,
the one with the zinnia hairdo.
And the other sister swims across the bay, held up
by blue water. And her sister is drinking
quietly and desperately and continuously
in a northern oil town
and one of the children has fallen off the window ledge.
So the other sister swims with slow determination
from one end of the bay to the other.
It is a matter of liquids,
it is a matter of being held up,
it is a matter of not falling,
it is a matter of keeping on with the swimming motions.

One sister died in the bombardments
and the other sister refugeed with her children
to the countryside. One sister married a tall dark man
and went underground for six months

because she ate his seed, and she liked it,
and zinnias sprouted out of her mouth like words.
Three sisters died in the riots in the square
and the last sister made it to the countryside with
two mattresses, three blankets, four children
and a water container.
One sister married a tall dark man and went underground,
the other sister did not marry a tall dark man
and went underground anyway.
A hundred sisters died in the siege and a few made it
to the countryside and married tall dark men and they all
lived underground.
A thousand thousand thousand thousand sisters died
in the fires and the falling buildings
along with their fathers and their brothers
and their uncles and their mothers
and their children and their cousins
and their neighbours
and the unborn
and the unborn
and the unborn.

SONG TO THE RISING SUN

(Dedicated to Caroline Woodward)

1

What did we do all winter while we waited for the sun?
It was gone such a long time.
Our thoughts grew too vague to contain.
What did we do all that winter in the Arctic while we waited for
    the sun?
The stars never stopped looking down at us.
What did we do as we moved into the precise and surgical cold of
    January?
What did we do?

We listened to the radio, we listened to the seductive
and fraudulent voices,
we listened to the voices of pilots overhead in the dark,
we listened for the call sign of the criminal devils
at the Black Angel Lead and Zinc Mine,
we watched with fascination and dread
the talking heads of television from distant places,
we drew up plans,
we cut our losses,
we re-read our contracts,
we visited everybody in the village,
we dreamed,
we were dreamed,
we looked again and again at the northern mountains
behind the village
where the sun would come up,
we talked ourselves out of despair,

we deceived each other,
we traded clothes,
we ran the huskies out from under the staff house,
we wrote eyewitness reports,
we wrote appeals to get our friends out of jail in Kuujuuak,
we invented relationships,
we became deft and scandalous,
we listened to the breaking and the cannonades
of the moving ice,
the destruction of ice at the shear zone,
we arose in the dark and saw angels walking with candles
under the landfast ice, through the caves and tunnels
under the landfast ice,
we watched beings walking down from the northern
mountains in glowing zodiacal bituminous fires,
beautiful and shoeless,
we lay back in our beds, starfire descending.
The spirit sings.
The spirit sings.
The spirit also weeps.

2

I have been trying to reach you by radio all winter
but the air is full of darkness,
telepresences, moving stones, talking heads, wizards,
devices, shaky people moving without hands,
devices, radio waves, refuelling aircraft.
I sit up late, listening to Shaman Radio.
The seductive and fraudulent voices tell me of murders
in far places, committed with enthusiasm and skill.
I do not know why the human mind pauses in
the darknesses it does.
But mine has as well.
I drink so deeply of the crystalline and windless stillness
but there is no still place for this thirst.

3

When I first came up here
I came up on a Twin Otter, a cargo plane
carrying four barrels of aviation fuel.
I like living on the edge.
We flew over the Black Angel Lead and Zinc Mine
at 8,000 feet,
and the stories the pilot told me were always full of money.
Junk is lethal.
We flew through a thickening, dirty pollution haze
that comes up from the megacities.
Junk is lethal.
He said once his cargo door flew open and he lost
all these boxes of apples
over the Davis Straits,
and he said, you know,
I think Big Stuff will save us.

4

I am trying to reach you by radio.
Listen. Take thought, take thought, think. Listen. Watch.
I am trying to reach you by radio telephone,
waiting for the sun to come back.
I wanted to tell you
we don't have very long.
We are losing things.
There is a black hole in the ionosphere
out of which lost things are going.
We dreamed.
We were dreamed.
I became far too involved with the man
who was ruined; who had a love of
intrigue and whiskey, as did I; lost things are going.
There are 100 million tons of sulphur dioxide
staining the polar air
into a haze that pilots cannot fly through.
Junk is lethal.
We are waiting out the long Arctic night.
The air is overloaded with signals.
In the eastern Arctic, the air is dirty with signals.
Brand names, long wave, short wave, the morse of
supply ships coming up the Davis Strait with their cargoes
of summer fuel
and dreaming sailors
dreaming up the long straits
and the heart's charged cargo spills the entire load out
8,000 feet over the Davis Straits
spilling its dirty hearts, and the
haunting, flaccid little poems we all used to write.
Junk is lethal.

Junk is lethal.

What you really want is whatever is really big and comes
from someplace else that isn't here and can only be oper-
ated by trained experts and is made up of complex com-
ponents that can only be repaired in Zurich and displaces
trillions of cubic feet and is image-intensified at a rate
of twenty thousand pounds per square inch and can deal
with four thousand feet of unconsolidated sediments and
the buildup in terms of p.s.i. whatever has digital read-
outs. yes. yes. yes. yes. it has to have digital readouts.

Wake up and start again.
Wake up and free yourself.
You must be told this over and over, in dreams,
in messages, in radio waves.
There is more than this, even though the darkness
is seductive with points of light,
snow refractions,
even though there are angels walking under the landfast ice;
you are sick with power
you are sick with the deep acids of power
heavy metals washing ashore,
even though there are beautiful and shoeless people
moving in bituminous fires through the aurora borealis,
even though the legendary stars move in circles
around the high centred polestar
there is more than this. There is more than this long night.
You must be told this over and over.
Wake up. Wake up. Look to the northern mountains,
look beyond the river of Salluit,
look beyond the Kuujuuak, the Povungnirtuk,
Big Stuff will not save us. Wake up. Look. Keep watch.

5

You were promised something.
You were promised that the sun would come back
out of the long Arctic night.
You were promised clear air, clean water.
It was promised that you would be loved
and they owe you, remember that.
Listen to Shaman Radio, listen
to this seductive and fraudulent voice;
they promised you the way the sun makes promises
to the moon
even when the moon is on the opposite side of the world
even when the moon has gone down into the running stains
of the Black Angel Lead and Zinc Mine
even though the sun has abandoned us and left us
in darkness for so long,
promises like the cheerful kisses
of the saffron poppies of the Ungava.
Trust yourself, says the invisible sun, trust me,
trust the light that may rise within you all winter
time after time
following the route of the invisible sun
the moon our representative
the refuelling aircraft arriving on the sea ice,
trust yourself and the light that may rise within you
beautiful and shoeless
down the long alleys of ice at the shear zone
the glitter of accumulated village snow,
and everything I saw in the Arctic and everything I did
became a part of me.

This is my body of darkness and this is my cargo of light.
I was heavy with my body of darkness,
I ride with my cargo of light.

6

And what are the standards set for this sunlight
that has been promised us?
That it be clear.
That it be freely given.
That it fall on everybody at the same time.
That it open our hearts of darkness.
That it illuminate the caves under the landfast ice.
That it give solar power to angels.
That it rise instantaneously over the rim of the northern mountains,
that it burst like floodwater down the fjord,
that it set alight and inflame the broken ice at the shear zone,
that it repair and mend our angry, flaccid little hearts,
that it ignite the plankton under the sea ice,
that it make the poppies flare and glitter on the stone tundra,
that it bring the huskies out from under the staff house,
that it draw the birds forward on their great migrations,
that it signal the caribou of the dwindling Ungava herd,
that they shake themselves,
that the hair fly up around them in a bright luminous cloud
as they shake themselves
and prepare to cross the rapids of the Kuujuuak,
that it turn on cloud-shadows over the opening sea,
that it awaken love and foxes.
These are the standards of sunlight.

7

And so we drift out of the precise, surgical cold of January.
We had been dreamed alive,
out of the wreck of the future
out of the violence of opposites
our dreams washing over us all the Arctic night like the tides
under the landfast ice,
running up the Ungava coast in foam and black salt
the routines of oppressive and heavy metals
the heavy metals now in our flesh
now and forever in our flesh
and in the flesh of our people,
and in the flesh of the animals we have dreamed.

8

We always knew we were somebody else
as well as the people we have become.
Something is dreaming us, as persons of intelligent purity,
an evocative and spontaneous self.
We would like to meet this self
in a landscape with Arctic herb-willow blossoms
and the saffron northern poppies
and peregrine falcons overhead,
their airy voices light as shortwave,
walking through these dreams in mortal terror
here on the planet of our birth
here in this polar region
we live through profound experiences
every moment of our lives
every second of our lives,
and we do not know it.
You are right to live in fear.

9

We have to walk on earth as if we lived here.
There is no help for it.
Even if we can only pretend we live here.
They are a small people, but hardy and truthful.
Moving on faith alone.
In the hot moonlight and drifting black shadows,
you are right to live in joy, but
do not meddle in the ways of wizards
for they are subtle,
and quick to anger.

10

And every dream is an explorer's map recovered at great cost
and every map is a chart for land-dancing,
and every river is a song driven by longing
but be still. Sit down here beside me.
Look at the northern mountains,
because this is the opening chord of the music,
because even the darkest heart can be opened,
because the sun can move across the limb of the south
without our help,
because the only changes we have made here
were the wrong ones,
because we have torn a hole in the ionosphere,
because we are pouring out 100 million tons
of sulphur dioxide a year,
because we have soaked the Arctic pole in a pollution haze
that pilots cannot fly through,
because we have blamed it on everybody else,
because we have said poetry will be only
small lyrics of pastoral love,
because this Arctic sun will open your body on its rising,
because your heart is the sun of the world,
because the sun rises and rises over the bare mountains,
the tundra,
the iron cross on the mountain of Salluit,
because the peregrine falcons are coming back,
their airy voices light as shortwave,
because I am trying to reach you by radio,
and because in the heart of this midnight
there is a sun of the upper air,
because of the bituminous fires, the beings beautiful
and footloose,

because the sun is arriving over the bright ice of the fjord,
because it was promised us that it would rise,
because we were torn apart into lightness
and dark in our original natures,
because we were torn in half,
because the rising recreates us,
because the rising recreates us
just this second
and no more.

BIBLIOGRAPHY

Waterloo Express. Toronto: House of Anansi, 1973.

The Golden Hawks. Toronto: James Lorimer, 1976, 1985.

Celestial Navigation. Toronto: McClelland & Stewart, 1984.

The Late Great Human Road Show. Vancouver: Talon Books, 1986.

Sitting in the Club Car Drinking Rum and Karma Cola. Winlaw: Polestar Press, 1986 (now in 8th printing).

The Jesse James Poems. Winlaw: Polestar Press, 1986.

Blackwater. New York: Knopf, 1988.

Song to the Rising Sun. Winlaw: Polestar Press, 1989.

Cousins. New York: Knopf, forthcoming September, 1991.

ANTHOLOGIES (SELECTED)

Sullivan, Rosemary, editor. *Poetry by Canadian Women*. Toronto: Oxford, 1989.

Scheier, Libby, Sheard, Sarah, & Wachtel, Eleanor, editors. *Language in Her Eye: Writing and Gender*. Toronto: Coach House Press, 1990.

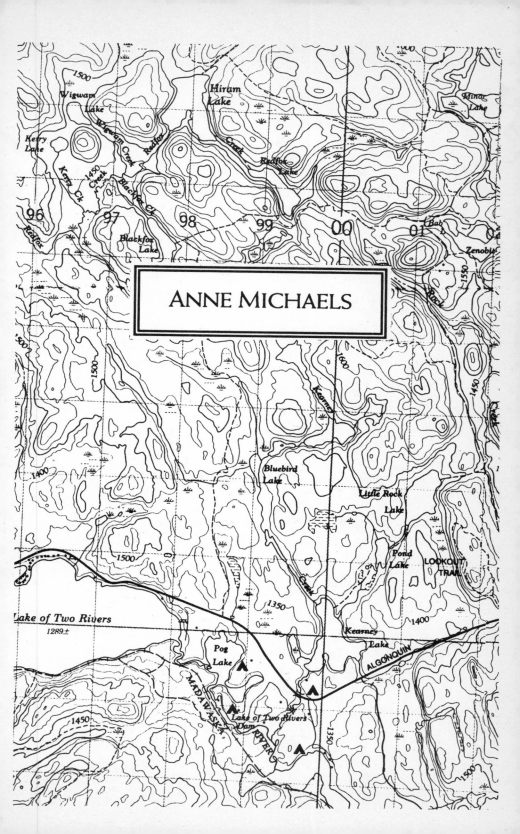

ANNE MICHAELS

UNSEEN FORMATIONS

"The word is a small visible portion of a
gigantic unseen formation."
— Peter Brook

1

A FEW YEARS AGO SCIENTISTS reached into the frozen ground on
Axel Heiberg Island in the Arctic, and pulled up handfuls of fresh
leaves, forty-five million years old. Twigs were strewn on a fossil
forest floor — redwood and water fir fresh enough to be broken
and burned — as if they'd waited millions of years to be gathered
up for fire.

When you're elbow-deep in time and pull your hand out, drip-
ping with images that seem older than your own experience, that's

173

the moment of the poem. Prose uses the extended image, the scene, while poetry relies on the metaphor, the image imbedded in contexts. The metaphor guides the poet down the twisting and sudden neural paths between conscious and unconscious, between personal and social, between memory and meaning. Without it the poem remains mired in the self; the lights are out, the poem stays dark.

Like a landscape, the poem is a cross-section, an archeological/geological slice: its density must reflect layers of time as well as meaning. Every landscape is a narrative: the static surface is an illusion, and actually reveals all the earth forces that forged and continue to forge the present geological moment. That's why the metaphor is crucial to me: the density of contexts rubbing against each other is the thrum of the mutable world. If a poem can be thought of as attempting to clone an emotional, intellectual, and visceral event, then it's the metaphor that serves as the genetic key to the whole organism; that's one way poems can seem to contain "everything," cloned from the single cell of a present moment. Lives and landscapes rise from their histories. The poem, attempting to seize a present moment, reveals the force of time. For this reason, and because poetry is intensity of language (a line is not a sentence, no matter how tightly or loosely packed), I aim for density — and hope for a unified and singing surface. (In fact, if a poem is constructed just right, you can almost read it effectively from bottom to top.) Not surprisingly, I explore events through geology, natural history as well as biography, history. At any given moment — say, in the elusive dream stillness of an August afternoon — the ground could give way and you could find yourself tumbling down a primal mine. The title of my last book, *Miner's Pond* — tries to hint that being able to see the water's surface and down to the bottom at the same time — the present moment and the past — are of equal importance. The significance of a present moment is *not* that it is a gate to the past, but that it takes its place in a signifi-

174

cant, mysterious narrative. Reaching back, like looking at stars, the poem is illumined by forward light.

2

A real power of words is that they make our ignorance more precise. Writing is negative aspiration: to work strenuously towards the moment when failure is confirmed. For minutes, sometimes even months after "completing" a poem, the writer can believe she's glimpsed knowledge larger than her own experience. Then the gleam is covered over with sand, and the writer settles for a fact far less grandiose — that after all the work, perhaps one knows something more than before. Writing is a desperate act, in the sense that one always knows it will end in failure. What's on the page is only an entry point for what's still buried in ourselves. A shred, a shadow. Truth is guarded by the impeccable security system of the uncertainty principle: the poem is the trail in the cloud chamber.

*

The "perfect" intensity of a short poem is an ideal: concision that heightens complexity, without obscurity or reduction, a glint of profundity both visceral and intellectual, in language that brands itself into memory, musical and charged. This is an ideal so far out of reach it makes my head ache and my limbs nervous. The truly perfect short poem, one that seems to achieve everything, is so out of reach, it safely occupies the realm of delusion in terms of my own ambitions. Not that the long poem isn't fraught with dangers; the challenge of maintaining a taut singing tension over the course of a not truly linear narrative; each line packed like a lyric. An attempt to achieve horizontal flow and vertical descent at the same time, seeming effortless as a river searing its way through hills over time. How to do this, so that the poem doesn't dry up or get tangled with grasses or freeze? For me, it takes an average of four years for a long poem to reveal itself; one must wait for every connecting image and metaphor to rise organically from the themes; large themes are revealed through small details: these details either push up or the landscape they're embedded in erodes; the poem emerges. As in painting, whether one is applying pigment or gouging, each stroke is for depth. The ways in which a poem completes itself, the triggers and accidents of discovery are always surprising. And just as every landscape continues to form itself, the writer fantasizes that the poem continues to change, in the reader's experience. A slow process of writing that embraces months not days is immensely satisfying. There's the erotic pleasure of prolonged passion: only when you completely surrender to your material will your material surrender to you. But perhaps more important, this patience embraces the two extremes of a writing life. Writing is often described in terms that set it apart from "real life" — requiring either monastic self-discipline and dispassionate observation on one hand, or manic intensity on the other. If writing requires both extremes, the only moderator is time. A long rhythm that encompasses months and years instead of days allows less artificial distinction between "work" and "life."

It also allows time for the ego to struggle with the humility of accepting preordained defeat.

3

The brain is in the body and the body is in the brain: a poem gets "under the skin" through content, sound and rhythm. For me, the best writing doesn't let me forget the body for too long, the way the best theology binds us to the earth, to the mysteries and responsibilities of our mortality. Some poems have the power to remember us, and these are the ones we return to, like holy sites. Rare words that make wisdom and music inseparable from breath. It's been said that poetry is a response to silence, and in some sense that's true; as John Berger wrote: "to break the silence of events, to speak of experience however bitter or lacerating, to put into words, is to discover the hope that these words may be heard, and that when heard, the events will be judged ...." I think that the most fulfilling poetry goes one step further, returning the reader into silence, into the privacy of wordlessness, a leap back into the body. When I write, one of my wishes is to eventually push the reader from the page, to lift her head from the book until she looks again at the faces she loves.

Language casts a wide net; you capture something only by pulling up a lot of dross with it; the shell still entangled with seaweed. A "truth" is always mired in personal context, the way weather inhabits a room.

4

In some traditions, history is told always as if in the present; the present generation is never considered apart from its ancestors. Always "we," not "they": "When *we* were exiled from Egypt ... " The poet collapses time in the same way, whether an event invented to have happened in the past or one imagined in a future. All poems exist in the present, as we pull them dripping with failure from their hiding places in the world.

*

When my mother told me stories about her grandmother, a woman well-loved in her community for her good works, a woman whose generosity and energy were talked about long after her death, the lesson my mother wanted to impart was obvious: actions speak louder than words — the food delivered to an ill neighbour, the hours of comfort and support. But another message was equally obvious: without my mother's words, her grandmother's life, her good deeds, her story, would soon have faded from memory. So the knot was tied and continues to tighten in my own life: not action instead of words, but rather, action and words. Writing is one kind of giving. To become what you wish to give, quite another.

Save us from the writer who claims she's speaking for anyone other than herself; no writer speaks for her tribe, only from her place in it. What gives power to a poet's words is not, for example, her attempt to sum up a corrupt political system by speaking on behalf of a particular group, but instead to say simply: this is what I see. When the Russian poet Anna Akhmatova was asked that famous question while waiting with hundreds of others outside the Leningrad prison, everyone hoping for news of unjustly arrested friends or family (victims of a Stalinist purge), she was not asked — although known as a great poet and a heroic dissident — "will you speak for us?", but rather, and more rightly, she was asked: "Can you describe this?"

For a citizen who acts and a writer who spends periods of time cloistered from society, the dilemma is the same; the dilemma of the witness. Not only: Who am I to say? but also: Who am I, if I don't say. The more deeply you examine your own life, the more deeply you enter your times, and from there, history. And if one is compelled to examine the overwhelming cruelty of her age, the simple directive — "can you describe this?" — becomes an impossible task of even greater magnitude than language's ordinary failure, because morality is dependent on its accuracy. As for the answering voices of pleasure and gratitude, they too take on a "moral" imperative, as the other essential extreme of the "truth."

Some writing redeems lost chances. What a private grace — that in the white dimension of the page, there's a room thick with the weather of irony, loud with words never spoken; where ideological or metaphysical or physical passions have been pulled taut over time, significant moments eternally fraying thin with intensity. Like the archeologist reaching into cold Arctic ground to a fresh forest millions of years old, we dig into the past with the aim of pulling up the future, handfuls of possibility, words to burn. And in aiming for the future, just maybe we succeed in naming a present moment, fresh and already burning.

❖

BIOGRAPHICAL NOTE

Anne Michaels' first book, The Weight of Oranges, *won the Commonwealth Prize for the Americas in 1986. Her articles, reviews and interviews have appeared in numerous magazines. Currently she teaches writing at the University of Toronto.*

LAKE OF TWO RIVERS

1

Pull water, unhook its seam.

Lie down in the lake room,
in the smell of leaves still sticky from their birth.

Fall to sleep the way the moon falls
from earth: perfect lethargy of orbit.

2

Six years old, half asleep,
a traveler. The night car mysterious
as we droned past uneasy twisting fields.

My father told two stories on these drives.
One was the plot of "Lost Horizon,"
the other: his life.
This speeding room, dim in the dashboard's green emission,
became the hijacked plane carrying Ronald Colman to Tibet,
or the train carrying my father across Poland in 1931.

Spirit faces crowded the windows of a '64 Buick.
Unknown cousins surrounded us, arms around each other,
a shawl of sleeves.

The moon fell into our car from Grodno.

It fell from Chaya-Elke's village,
where they stopped to say goodbye.
His cousin Mashka sat up with them
in the barn, while her face
floated down the River Neman in my father's guitar.
He watched to remember
in the embalming moonlight.

3

Sensate weather, we are your body,
your memory. Like a template,
branch defines sky, leaves
bleed their gritty boundaries,
corrosive with nostalgia.

Each year we go outside to pin it down,
light limited, light specific,
light like a name.

*

For years my parents fled at night,
loaded their children in the back seat,
a tangle of pyjamas anxious to learn the stars.

I watched the backs of their heads
until I was asleep, and when I woke
it was day, and we were in Algonquin.

I've always known this place,
familiar as a room in our house.

The photo of my mother, legs locked in water,
looking into the hills where you and I stand —

only now do I realize
it was taken before I was born.

*

Purple mist, indefinite hills.

At Two Rivers, close as branches.
Fish scatter, silver pulses with their own electric logic.

Milky spill of moon over the restless lake,
seen through a sieve of foliage.

In fields to the south
vegetables radiate underground,
displace the earth.
While we sit, linked by firelight.

4

The longer you look at a thing
the more it transforms.

My mother's story is tangled,
overgrown with lives of parents and grandparents
because they lived in one house and among them
remembered hundreds of years of history.

This domestic love is plain, hurts
the way light balancing objects in a still life hurts.

The heart keeps body and spirit in suspension,
until density pulls them apart.
When she was my age
her mother had already fallen through.

Pregnant, androgynous with man,
she was afraid. When life goes out,
loss gets in, wedging a new place.

Under dark lanes of the night sky
the eyes of our skin won't close,
we dream in desire.
Love wails from womb, caldera, home.
Like any sound, it goes on forever.

*

The dissolving sun turns Two Rivers into skin.
Our pink arms, slightly fluorescent,
hiss in the dusky room, neon tubes bending
in the accumulated dark.

Night transforms the lake into a murmuring solid.
Naked in the eerie tremor of leaves rubbing stars,
in the shivering fermata of summer,
in the energy of stones made powerful by gravity,
desire made powerful by the seam between starlight and skin,
we join, moebius ribbon in the night room.

5

We do not descend, but rise from our histories.
If cut open memory would resemble
a cross-section of the earth's core,
a table of geographical time.
Faces press the transparent membrane
between conscious and genetic knowledge.
A name, a word, triggers the dilatation.
Motive is uncovered, sharp overburden in a shifting field.

*

When I was twenty-five I drowned in the River Neman,
fell through when I read that bone-black from the ovens
was discarded there.

Like a face pressed against a window,
part of you waits up for them,
like a parent, you wait up.

*

A family now, we live each other's life
without the details.

The forest flies apart, trees are shaken loose
by my tears,

by love that doesn't fall to earth
but bursts up from the ground, fully formed.

MINER'S POND

in memory of Elie David Michaels

1

A caver under stalactites,
the moon searches the stars.

In the low field, pools turn to stone.
Starlight scratches the pond,
penetrates in white threads;
in a quick breath, it fogs into ice.
A lava of fish murmurs the tightening film.

The crow is darkness's calculation;
all absence in that black moment's ragged span.

*

Above Miner's Pond, geese break out of the sky's
pale shell. They speak non-stop, amazed
they've returned from the stars,
hundreds of miles to describe.

It's not that they're wild, but
their will is the same as desire.
The sky peels back under their blade.

Like a train trestle, something in us rattles.
All November, under their passing.

*

Necks stiff as compass needles,
skeletons filled with air;
osmosis of emptiness, the space in them
equals space.

Their flight is a stria, a certainty;
sexual, one prolonged
reflex.

Cold lacquering speed, feathers oiled by wind,
surface of complete transfluency.
The sky rides with tremors in the night's milky grain.

*

Windows freeze over like shallow ponds,
hexagonally blooming.
The last syrup of light boils out from under the lid
of clouds; sky the colour of tarnish.
Like paperweights, cows hold down the horizon.

Even in a place you know intimately,
each night's darkness is different.

They aren't calling down to us.
We're nothing to them, unfortunates
in our heaviness.
We watch at the edge of words.

At Miner's Pond we use the past
to pull ourselves forward; rowing.

2

It was the tambourine that pushed my father
over the edge in 1962. His patience
a unit of time we never learned to measure.
The threat to "drive into a post"
was a landmark we recognized and raced towards
with delirious intent,
challenging the sound barrier of the car roof.

We were wild with stories we were living.
The front seat was another time zone
in which my parents were imprisoned, and from which
we offered to rescue them, again and again.

That day we went too far.
They left us at the side of the road
above St. Mary's quarry. My mother insists
it was my father's idea, she never wanted to drive away,
but in retrospect, I don't believe her.

This was no penalty; drilled in wilderness protocol,
happy as scouts, my brothers
planned food and shelter.
The youngest, I knew they'd come back for us,
but wasn't sure.

Hot August, trees above the quarry like green flames,
dry grass sharpened by the heat, and
dusty yellow soil "dry as mummy skin,"
a description meant to torment me.

They were rockhounds howling in the plastic light
melting over fossil hills,
at home among eras.

It was fifteen minutes, maybe less,
and as punishment, useless.
But the afternoon of the quarry lives on,
a geological glimpse,
my first grasp of time,
not continuous present.

*

Their language took apart landscapes,
stories of sastrugi and sandstreams,
shelves and rain shadow.
Atoms vibrating to solids,
waves into colours. Everything stone
began to swirl. Did the land sink
or the sea rise? When my brothers told me
I'd never seen the stars, that light's too slow,
that looking up is looking back,
there was no holding on. Beyond my tilting room
night swarmed with forest eyes and flying rats,
insects that look like branches, reptiles like rocks.
Words like solfatara, solfatara,
slipping me down like terraced water, into sleep.

*

Full of worlds they couldn't keep to themselves,
my brothers were deviant programmers of nightmares.
Descriptions of families *just like ours,*

with tongues petrified and forks welded to their teeth,
who'd sat down to Sunday dinner
and were flooded by molten rock;
explorers gnawing on boots in the world's dark attic;
Stadacona's sons, lured onto Cartier's ship and held hostage,
never to see home again.

When the lights were out
my free will disappeared.
Eyes dry with terror, I plummeted
to the limbo of tormented sisters, that global sorority
with chapters in every quiet neighbourhood, linked by fear
of volcanic explosions and frostbite, polar darkness,
and kidnapping by Frenchmen.

*

The ritual walk to the bakery, Fridays
before supper. Guided by my eldest brother
through streets made unfamiliar by twilight,
a decade between us.
I learned about invisibility:
the sudden disappearance of Röntgen's skin —
his hand gone to bones — and the discovery of X-rays.
Pasteur's germs, milk souring on the doorsteps of Arbois,
and microbe-laden wine — "what kind of wine?" —
the word "microbe"
rolling in my brother's 14-year-old mouth
like an outstanding beaujolais.
On these walks, frogs came back to life with electricity.
Sheep were cured of sheep-sickness.
Father Time, Einstein, never wore a watch.
Galileo saw the smooth face of the moon

instantly grow old,
more beautiful for being the truth.
The Curies found what they'd been looking for
only after giving up; they opened the lab and saw the glow,
incorruptible residue, radiant stain!

In winter, Glenholme Avenue was already dark,
with glass trees, elms shivering in their ice-sleeves.
As we walked, the essence of fresh bread
whirled into the secular air,
the street hungry for its pure smell.

Even now, I wrap what's most fragile
in the long gauze of science.
The more elusive the truth,
the more carefully it must be carried.

Remembering those walks,
I think of Darwin —
"no object in nature could avoid his loving recognition" —
on the bunk of the Beagle,
green with sea-sickness and the vertigo
of time. He was away five years
but the earth aged by millions.
Greeting him at Falmouth dock, his father cried:
"Why the shape of his head has changed!"
Stepping from cold night into the bright house,
I knew I'd been given privileged information,
because the excitement in my brother's voice
was exclusive to the street, temporary,
a spell.

*

Brother love, like the old family boat
we call the tin can: dented, awkward,
but still able to slice the lake's pink skin.

*

A family is a study in plate-tectonics, flow-folding.
Something inside shifts; suddenly we're closer or apart.

There are things brothers and sisters know —
the kind of details a spy uses
to prove his identity —
fears that slide through childhood's long grass,
things that dart out later; and pleasures like toucans,
their brightness weighing down the boughs.
Who but a brother calls from another hemisphere
to read a passage describing the strange
blip in evolution, when reptiles looked like
"alligator-covered coffee tables,"
evolution's teenagers, with a "severe case of the jimjams
during the therapsid heyday" —
remembering those were the creatures we loved best,
with bulky limbs and backs like sails.

Memory is cumulative selection.
It's an undersea cable connecting one continent
to another,
electric in the black brine of distance.

3

Migrating underground, miles below the path of the geese,
currents and pale gases
stray like ghosts through walls of rock.
Above and below, the way is known;
but here, we're blind.

The earth means something different now.
It never heals, upturned constantly.

Now stones have different names.

Now there's a darkness like the lakes of the moon;
you don't have to be close to see it.

*

My brother's son lived
one fall, one spring.

We're pushed outside, towards open fields,
by the feeling he's trying to find us.

Overhead the geese are a line,
a moving scar. Wavering
like a strand of pollen on the surface of a pond.
Like them, we carry each year in our bodies.
Our blood is time.

WHAT THE LIGHT TEACHES

*"I break open stars and find nothing and again nothing,
and then a word in a foreign tongue."*
— Elisabeth Borcher

1

Countless times this river has been bruised by our bodies;
liquid fossils of light.

We shed our ghost skins in the current;
then climb the bank, heavy and human.

The river is a loose tongue,
a folk song. At night we go down to listen.
Stars like sparks from a bonfire.
We take off what we are,
and step into the moon.

2

When there are no places left for us,
this is where we'll still meet.
Past the white fountain of birches,
green helmets of willows.
Past the boulder that fastens the field
like a button on a pocket.
Here, where trees you planted are now twice our height.

In winter we'll haunt your kitchen, our love
an overturned bowl, a circling lid.
We'll visit the creaking bog with its sunken masts;
fly over a death mask of snow
and the frozen pond striped with grass —
to our river, humming between closed lips.
Attentive as your favorite poet,
Tsvetaeva — who listened with the roots of her hair.

3

Birds plunge their cries like needles
into the thick arm of afternoon.

Beyond the closed window, soundless pines —
a heavy green brocade; and the glowing, stiff
brush cut of the corn.
Wands of wild calla.
Lilies tall as children.

You're asleep on the couch, head up, as if in a bath;
summer heat turns thin white sleeves
pink against your skin.
Sleeping as if you'd waited years
for a place to close your eyes.

Everything familiar:
dishes and smells, faces in oval wooden frames,
tins of Russian tea
with their forest scenes, their borders of black and gold,
lining the shelves.

We float in death,
the ordinary world holds together
like the surface tension of water,
still and stretched, a splash of light.
The shadow pattern of leaves,
a moving tattoo on your bare legs.

4

Sometimes I was afraid to touch him,
afraid my hand would go right through him.
But he was alive, in a history
made more painful by love.

I prayed to the sky to lift our father's head,
to deliver him from memory.

I wished he could lie down
in music he knew intimately, and become
sound, his brain flooded by melody so powerful
it would stretch molecules, dismantle thought.

5

Suspended in flux, in contortions of disorder,
in the frozen acrobatics of folding and faults,
the earth mourns itself.
Continents torn in half and turned into coastlines,
call for themselves across the sea.
Caves, frantic for air, pull themselves up
by the ground, fields collapsing into empty sockets.
Everywhere the past juts into the present;
mountains burst from one era to another,
or crumple up millennia, time joining at its ends.

We also pleat time.
Remembering, we learn to forget.
The kind of forgetting that stops us, one foot
in the spring soil of your farm,
the other in mud where bits of bone and teeth
are still suspended, a white alphabet.
The kind of forgetting that changes
moonlight on the river into shreds of skin.
The forgetting that is the heart's
filthy drain,
so fear won't overflow its deep basin.

Even in its own confusion,
in its upheavals and depressions,
the earth has room in its heart.
Carefully, part by part, it replaces us.
Gently, so bones may embrace a little longer,
mud replaces marrow.

The dogs slip like mercury through the long grass.

How can we but feel they're here,
in the strange darkness of a thermosensitive sky,
even as light gushes over rocks
and the sun drips sweet fat the colour of peaches
over fields. Here, in the noise of the river,
a mother gives birth in a sewer;
soldiers push sand down a boy's throat.

Theirs are voices we hear
but can't hear, like the silence
of parents rounded up in a town square,
who stopped their tongues in time,
saving children by not calling them in the street.

Our father's daughters, we can't dream ourselves
into another world, see things differently.
Instead, we try to withstand memory
with memory, to go back further, to before:
back to the dacha in the high forests of Kochtobel,
to the Moyka in our mother's silvery photo of Petersburg,
to the wooden sidewalks of Kiev.
You read poems in the old language
even our parents can't speak —
what we save, saves us —
and in your mouth the soft buzzes are natural as cicadas,
the long "ayas" like bird calls.

Language is how ghosts enter the world.
They twist into awkward positions
to squeeze through the black spaces.
The dead read backwards,
as in a mirror. They gather
in the white field and look up,
waiting for someone
to write their names.

Language remembers.
Out of obscurity, a word takes its place
in history. Even a word so simple
it's translatable: number. Oven.

Because all change is permanent,
we need words to raise ourselves
to new meaning: tea and dacha and river.

6

It stopped me, the first time
I looked out at our father in the yard and saw
how she leaned her head on his shoulder —
familiar, and full of desire.

Together they looked at a nest in the bushes,
inspected strawberries.
Although the air was humid with lilacs,
heavy with insects and rain,
she was cool in a dress the colour of the moon.

You were reading by the open door.
The sound of a lawn mower made everything still.
Then a moment like night cereus
that blooms only in the dark, waking us
with its alarm of scent.

It wasn't seeing your face so suddenly like his,
or the sight of death in her white dress;
or the glaze of summer light
hardening into crust. Not the accustomed sadness
of what we'd lost,
but a new injury, a gash
bleeding into everything:
what we were losing.

7

When there are no places left for us,
we'll still talk in order to make things true:
not only the years before we were born,
not only the names of our dead,
but also this life.
The simple feel of an apple in the hand.
The look of the table after a meal, *en déshabillé*,
rings of wine like lips staining the cloth,
the half-eaten fish in its halo of lemon and butter.
Nights of tastes, of different smoothnesses;
nights when the twister of desire touches down
and tears up sleep;
of drowning in the shadow of your own body.

But if memory is only skin,
if we become dervishes spinning
at the speed of the world, feeling
nothing,
we spend hours by the river, telling everything.
So that when we are gone, even our spirits
weighed down with stones,
the river will remember.

8

It was a suicide mission, to smuggle language
from mouths of the dying
and the dead; last words of the murdered mothers —
Germany, Poland, Russia.
They found that what they'd rescued
wasn't the old language at all;
only the alphabet the same.
Because language of a victim only reveals
the one who named him.

Because they were plucked from the centre,
because they shared the same table, same street,
there was no idiom to retreat to.

What was left but to cut out one's tongue,
or cleave it with new language,
or try to hear a language of the dead,
who were thrown into pits, into lakes —
What are the words for earth, for water?

The truth is why words fail.
We can only reveal by outline,
by circling absence.
But that's why language
can remember truth when it's not spoken.
Words in us that deafen,
that wait, even when their spell seems
wasted,
even while silence
accumulates to fate.

Prayer is the effort of wresting words
not from silence,
but from the noise of other words.
To penetrate heaven, we must reach
what breaks in us.
The image haunts me:
the double swaying
of prayer on the trains.

9

Whole cities were razed with a word.
Petersburg vanished into Leningrad, became
an invisible city where poets promised to meet
so they could pronounce again
"the blessed word with no meaning."

A writer buried his testimony
in the garden, black type in black soil,
trusting that someday earth would speak.
All those years of war and uncertainty after,
no one knew the power of his incantation,
calling quietly from its dark envelope.
From his notebook grew orchids and weeds.

Words are powerless as love,
transforming only by taking us as we are.

Reading letters from Tsvetaeva to a friend
we cried together in your barn:
"you're the only one I have left."

After all these years I still feel closest to you
in the hours reserved for nightmares,
even in our distant bedrooms.
Because I know you're awake too,
if not this night, then another,
watching your husband's sleeping body
rise with breath.

10

For years I've driven towards you in spring rain,
storm sky of green marble,
slow traffic a caravan of swinging lanterns,
windshield wipers like clock hands.
Poems by Tsvetaeva on the seat beside me,
flowers in wet paper.

As the hours pass, the hard seeds in my heart
soften and swell as I think of your kitchen
with its stone floor
like a summer house in Peredelkino,
and of Mandelstam, exiled to Yelabuga on the Kama:
"if you must leave the city,
it's best to live near a river."

You fly out of the darkness at me,
twisting open the tin sky.

The thunderstorm becomes other storms:
darkness steeping like tea above Burnside Drive,
with its slippery crease of rusted leaves;
or the night on High Street, rain
streaming like milk down the windshield
the moment the streetlights clicked on.
I think of young Akhmatova,
under a black umbrella with Modigliani,
reading Verlaine in the Luxembourg.
All the languages they spoke —
Russian, Italian, French —
and still, their lovemaking was with roses!
Language not enough
for what they had to tell each other.

Never to lose this joy,
driving to one who awaits my arrival.
Soon I will be standing on your porch, dripping
with new memory, a thin dress soaked with May rain.

Rain that helps one past grow out of another.

11

Language is the house with lamplight in its windows,
visible across fields. Approaching, you can hear
music; closer, smell
soup, bay leaves, bread — a meal for anyone
who has only his tongue left.
It's a country; home; family:
abandoned; burned down; whole lines dead, unmarried.
For those who can't read their way in the streets,
or in the gestures and faces of strangers,
language is the house to run to;
in wild nights, chased by dogs and other sounds,
when you've been lost a long time,
when you have no other place.

There are nights in the forest of words
when I panic, every step into thicker darkness,
the only way out to write myself into a clearing,
which is silence.
Nights in the forest of words
when I'm afraid we won't hear each other
over clattering branches, over
both our voices calling.

In winter, in the hour
when the sun runs liquid then freezes,
caught in the mantilla of empty trees;
when my heart listens
through the cold stethoscope of fear,
your voice in my head reminds me
what the light teaches.
Slowly you translate fear into love,
the way the moon's blood is the sea.

BIBLIOGRAPHY

The Weight of Oranges. Toronto: Coach House Press, 1986.

The Weight of Oranges. Toronto: Music Gallery/Coach House Press Talking Book, 1989.

Miner's Pond. Toronto: McClelland & Stewart, 1991.

ANTHOLOGIES

Sullivan, Rosemary, editor. *Poetry by Canadian Women*. Toronto: Oxford, 1989.

Poets 88. Kingston: Quarry Press, 1988

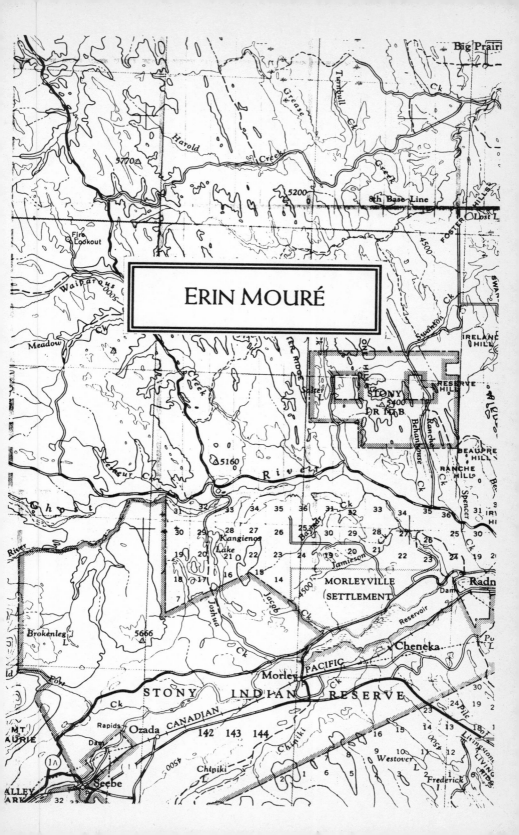

ERIN MOURÉ

AND POETRY /

A METHOD? IF ANYTHING, a kind of accretion. Sounds attract feel-
ings and aches, and vice versa. Sounds and words attract each other,
and ideas, and worries. And dreams. And the thread of remembrance
knitting the self over again, it's preposterous, it's hard to keep up
with, do justice to, keep track of. The world is imbued with lan-
guage and linguistic possibility, with bad and good expression, with
hopefulness, with manipulation and trickery as well, with rational-
izations and silence and gaps that alter, slowly, the structures of
thought in the head. And poetry laughs at all of this at the same
time as it confronts it, because poetry is entirely useless and owes
no debts. It's a weightless possession, at the same time bearing the
weight of responsibility and forgiveness. It's an object that is first
a noise, that is still and ever a noise, a resonance of words that alters
its noise over and over in the head, breaking through the pale corpse

of "the image" and "the self."

I revise a lot, and listen and learn when I am revising. And I try consciously to push words forward and make them tumble, to work through my own perceptual failures, to create a space/duration/marking where differences are possible, articulation that's multifaceted is possible. Break down the construct of the self, the seeing self, the self as un-self-conscious observer in the poem, as poetic voice!

As well, to me there's a relationship between physical processes, presence, and voice that is articulated only in relation to, that is constituted only in relation to *other beings*. Those links we have to each other, so well buried by the social constraints built into our speaking and perception. I'm more interested in the links, the movement of those linkages, than in "objects" or "conclusions" at either end. If you damage or conceal the links (as we do in damaging the earth or in underfunding AIDS hospices and medication), what are the consequences for the individual? I believe they are grave.

The structure of the poem? To me, absolute structure *is* motion. Structure as motion. Being is always in excess of this structure. *Remains* while the motion is, already past this place. Shock of that. Here we are. The body requires motion for memory. To explain context. Memory being only a part of the construct of a present context: that is, "the plausible." The brain puts forward plausibilities by selecting neural paths we have previously traveled. At the same time, the paths themselves "murmur," sign to each other. The paths alter themselves. Recontext is new context, then. Never the same. Requires motion. To be attentive outside the inner murmuring. Being *is* this attention "outside" in the midst of the murmur, attention to what is outer, to outer stimuli. The "identifiable." Speed. Burst of speed. "Furious."

I believe also "poetry is a limitless genre; its borders are only in ourselves and can be moved, in our lifetimes, if we dare to."

❖

BIOGRAPHICAL NOTE

Erin Mouré was born and raised in Calgary, Alberta. She attended the Universities of Calgary and British Columbia. She lived in Vancouver for ten years, since 1985 she lives and writes in Montreal. She has always worked in passenger rail and is presently at VIA Rail's headquarters in Montreal working in employee communications for the Customer Services department. In addition to her poetry, she writes essays, commentaries and reviews poetry from time to time in Books in Canada *and other publications. Her first book,* Empire, York Street, *was nominated for the Governor General's Award.* Domestic Fuel, *her third book, won the Pat Lowther Memorial Award.* Furious *won the 1988 Governor General's Award for Poetry.*

JUMP OVER THE GATE

I come home &
tell my mother I grew up.
I grew up! I say, & hug her.
Isn't it amazing! she says.
I go outside & open & slam
the door of the old refrigerator on the patio.
Our refrigerator!
Its round back like asthma, silent now;
a toque of snow over it.
Where did you come from? my mother says when I'm in.
I lay my mitts like two pages on the floor,
my boots dripping muddy smiles of water.
You! I say.

& she laughs. She's sitting at a high stool,
higher than the kitchen table,
paring an old soft cheese into a bowl.
I dip my hand in to taste.
It's good, I say.
Eat it on crackers! says my mother.

It bugs her most when I lean out the screen door
to call the dog out of the snow. Trix! I yell.
Puppy! I yell.
The dog is dead! my mother cries to me, but
I know she's still there in the yard.
Trix! I yell. We're going shopping!
Mom, I'm bringing the dog, I shout back to her.
Now the inside air is out, & vice versa,

it's cold.
Go ahead if that's what you like,
my mother sighs.
There should be a dog! I think.

Trix is with me & I let her run fast
& dip her head into the snow,
grabbing a big mouthful. She lopes ahead &
waits for me at the corners.
Cross! I yell.
& on the way back, I think:
if Trix were here she'd carry the package.
She liked to carry the package.
Trix! I yell for good measure.
Puppy! I yell for good measure.
When I get home, we both
jump over the gate.

You're back! my mother says.
There's really no Trix, I tell her;
& pass her the package, my boots scuffed with wet snow,
& pull the wool of my toque off my head.

I call her because I feel like it! I tell my mother.
I know! she says,
I know!

FIFTEEN YEARS

I am in a daydream of my uncle,
his shirt out at his daughter's wedding,
white scoop of the shirt-tail bobbing
on the dance floor.
When I think of it.
When I think of my cousin, otherwise,
shooting the BB gun up the exhaust pipe of his motorcycle,
behind the garage.
It is the softness of a puppy we have brought home from the farm,
& set on the grass to fall over crying,
sleeping in a boot next to the heart-tick of the alarm.

I am wondering how we live at all
unable to replace these images.
The green space beside my parents' house in summer
where we lay down on our stomachs to keep cool.
My uncle's shirt-tail beneath his suit jacket, dancing.
The flag of that shirt-tail.
I tell you.
His daughter married for fifteen years.

THIRTEEN YEARS

I am in a daydream of my uncle,
his shirt out at his daughter's wedding,
white scoop of the shirt-tail bobbing
on the dance floor & him in it, no,
his drunk friend pawing me, it was *his* shirt dangling,
I forgot this,
my youngest cousin in his dress pants downing straight whisky,
& me too, tying tin cans to his sister's car.
The sour taste of it. Drink this, he said.

I am wondering how we live at all
or if we do.
The puppy we grew up with came from the same uncle's farm.
His shirt-tail beneath his suit jacket, dancing.
The friend of the family touching my new chest.
They told me not to say so.
I'll drive you to the motel, he said, his breath close.
No. Be nice to him, they said, & waved me off from the table.
I was so scared.
Everyone had been drinking. Including me. Thirteen years old.
Who the hell did my cousin marry.
I tell you.

THE BEAUTY OF FURS

At lunch with the girls, the younger ones are talking about furs, &
what looks good with certain hair colours. Red fox looks no good
with my hair, says one. White fox looks snobbish, beautiful but
snobbish, says another one. They talk about the pronunciation of
coyote. I think of my brother catching muskrat. I think of pushing
the drown-set into the weeds, the freezing water of the Elbow, the
brown banks & snow we lived with, soft smell of aspen buds not
yet coming out on the trees, & us in our nylon coats in the back-
yards of Elbow Park Estates, practically downtown, trapping. *Coy-
oh-tea*, the women say. In some places they say *Ky-oot* or *Ky-oht*, I
say, thinking of the country where my brother now lives, the moan
of coyotes unseen, calling the night sky. & me caught in the drown-
set so deeply, my breath snuffled for years. & then it comes. They
are talking about the beauty of furs, and how so-and-so's family is
in the business. I remember, I say, I remember my mother had a
muskrat coat, & when she wore it & you grabbed her too hard by
the arm, fur came out. Eileen, fifteen years older than me, starts to
laugh, & puts her hand on my shoulder, laughing. We both start
laughing. I start to explain to her that it was old; my mother wore
it to church on Sunday & got upset if we grabbed her arm. We're
laughing so hard, now the young ones are looking at us, together
we are laughing, in our house there was a beaver coat like that Eileen
said, then suddenly we are crying, crying for those fur coats & the
pride of our mothers, our mothers' pride, smell of the coat at church
on Sunday, smell of the river, & us so small, our hair wet, kneeling
in that smell of fur beside our mothers

216

THE BEAUTY OF FURS: A Site Glossary

Later you realize it is a poem about being born, the smell of the fur is your mother birthing you & your hair is wet not slicked back but from the wetness of womb, the fur coat the hugest fur of your mother the cunt of your mother from which you have emerged & you cower in this smell The fur coat the sex of women reduced to decoration, & the womb the place of birth becomes the church in which you are standing, the womb reduced to decoration, where women are decoration, where the failure of decoration is the humiliation of women, to wear these coats, these emblems of their own bodies, in church on Sunday, children beside them The church now the place of birth & rebirth, they say *redemption*, everyone knows what this signifies & the mother is trying to pay attention, all the mothers, my mother, & we are children, I am children, a child with wet hair cowlick slicked down perfect, no humiliation, the site still charged with the smell of the river, the coat smell of the river, smell of the birth canal, caught in the drown-set is to be stopped from being born, is to be clenched in the water unable to breathe or see the night sky, the *coyohts* calling me upward, as if in these circumstances, so small beside my mother, I could be born now, but cannot, can I, because we are inside this hugest womb which has already denied us, in which we are decoration, in which men wear dresses & do the cooking, & the slicked hair is not the wet hair of birth but the hair of decoration, as if I could be born now, I am born, my snout warm smelling the wet earth of my mother's fur

TUCKER DRUGS

One hand clapping.
One hand feeling out the forehead bone of the skull, how
it protects the eyes with its overhang,
tectonic plate of the head, swivel neck beam over, at peripheral
    vision
edge, where the room jumps & flickers,
the window flies open or appears to,
people pick up their small briefcases & bubble hair
& jump into taxis,
drudgery, drudgery, the woman touching her forehead
where the light is, to turn it off & rest a bit,
rest the bone.

Our dog is whining.
Our dog is whining in the yard, its chain taut, hearing a sound none
    of us yet
imagine.
Four blocks away, my mother is opening the car
door, pulling out a bag, it tears & the drugstore paraphernalia,
shampoo & shoe liners, falls slowly to the pavement, oil-stained;
    someone
else comes out of the drug store looking at a picture magazine, bends
one page over,

this is what the dog hears, the print sliding forward off the page,
    the page bending,
the dog is howling louder now,
we expect my mother home any minute from Tucker Drugs
but the dog knows her car won't start, she won't come back

the dog howling so loud, it's stupid, we're not staying
here on the lawn chairs & that's it,

we get up & go in, & the door shuts, damn the howling dog.

NAMING A POEM CALLED TUCKER DRUGS

In which we don't know what weather it is.
"A poem in which the weather is not mentioned."
"A poem with a dog, a car, a drug store, and a mother in it."
"A poem in which there is not much weather."
"A poem in which the possible weather is limited by the presence
    of a consumer object."
"A poem with a dog in it."
"Tucker Drugs."

People may make a mistake if you call it this. With representation
   & naming being what they are, don't confuse people.

"A poem with Tucker Drugs in it."
"A poem using the words Tucker Drugs"
"A poem containing the provable geography of Tucker Drugs"
"A poem proving the writer has been to Calgary"
"A poem that will satisfy readers who have been to Tucker Drugs."

This is a patent lie. You can't name it this. People who have been to
Tucker Drugs may not be the kind of people who are satisfied to
read a poem containing the name of the drug store they have been in.

"A historical poem using Tucker Drugs."
"A poem in which a drug store struggles with its future as an image."
"A poem in which a drug store may end up in the title."
That's no good as a title.
"A poem in which the weather is not made apparent."
"A poem with a dog in it

"A poem with a woman's headache." "A poem written by a woman, in a woman's voice."

"A poem in which the window appears to fly open." "A poem in which no weather comes in

SEEBE

The mind's assumptive power
The assumptive power of the mind over the mind
The carrying of spit upward to the mouth on the end of a knife
this incredible spillage,

release of the river behind the dam at Seebe, recoil of water
rushing the gorge, where we have stood, our lines
taut connection between us & the water's surface, our blastular memory,
(t)autological

who we are, now, the spaces between words where time leaks out
& we are finished, finished, gone old;
the table of food finished & the guests left, & the spillage of glasses, &
our shirts empty, empty,

They say what saves the bones is weight-bearing exercise
except for the carrying of children
Which is our namesake,
which is what we do, naming

children,
taking their torsos in & out of the uterine wall
then carrying them, lifting
the weight of the small boy up from the side of the rails
& running forward to the train, stopped for us, his leg soft with blood
spattered my uniform, his leg not broken, just torn a bit at the skin,

This spillage, rusted gates pulled upward
to release the downstream blood
The mind's assumptive power of the Bow at Seebe
Carrying the boy to the conductor & then running back for the
kit, sunlit, "we hit a cow" they said in the lounge car afterward,
& me lifting the boy up from the dam where he was fishing,
the bridge where the whitefish run among the planted trout at Seebe

lifting him upward, his Stoney Indian face & bone weariness, watching
        me
white woman from the train taking him upward
into the vast, vast emptiness

Actually he was in the weeds
Actually he was nested hurt leg red in the weeds beside the train
so as not to be found again, got that?
All the tourists on the dam fishing sunlit maybe first hot weekend of
summer, delirium, delirium, trout dreams of the uterine memory, pulled
upward on the thin lines, water running high into the reservoir, oh Bow,
oh hotness,

we hit a cow, they said

The sudden yet soft emergency braking, pulling the cars up expert not too hard, we hit a cow they said in the curved light of the lounge at the end of it, & breaking out the side door lifting the green box, knowing nothing, knowing the sunlit heat on the back of the blue uniform, running down the right of way, the body not used to it yet, this gravelled running, the hot smell of spruce & light air of curious voices, the boys on the bridge having run, then; not knowing what would be found there, thinking of what to do in the bright run in the sun,

1) check breathing if you can find the mouth,
2) stop the bleeding,
3) immobilize fractures,

thinking the second step, going over it in the mind, so that when you look at someone completely bloody you see blood only where it is moving, it is the assumptive power of the mind, the mind over the mind, the deconstructive power of the human body, to take this, outward

He was in the weeds. & scared. He looked up soft at me. Hey, I say. You're okay. He was hiding there from me. I could see him. & ignored his hiding. Dropped the kit & bent over the torn leg. Bloody, that's all. Only one leg. The foot aligned well with the rest, okay, feeling up & down the bone, no, okay, just torn up & bleeding where? Here. Bleeding here. Okay. Lifting him up then & running carrying him back up to the train, the blue cars creaking, conductor, wait

give him up

& run back, the green kit just sitting tipped on the right of way, beside those weeds, grab it & run back, daring to look around at the trees & warm smell forest finally, jump back into the cars, we're off then

The poem has fallen apart into mere description.
It is years later, thinking of the mind's assumptive power & remembering the train hitting the boy at Seebe, Alberta & how I went out to get him. Here we have only my assumptions, only the arrogance of Erin Mouré made into the poem; in the course of history, which is description, the boy is mute. We have no way of entering into his images now. The description itself, even if questioned, portrays the arrogance of the author. In all claims to the story, there is muteness. The writer as witness, speaking the stories, is a lie, a liberal bourgeois lie. Because the speech is the writer's speech, and each word of the writer robs the witnessed of their own voice, muting them.

*Lifting him up, bone weary, taking him
into the vast, vast emptiness.*

NICE POETRY

there is a lot of hay in here

The "round hay bales." So many bales per field, so many
fields per quarter.
The line looks nice when we stop
before the preposition.
The field looks nice with the round bales of hay.

My brother puts his hand in the middle,
pulls out some threads of grass
puts them in his mouth
& chews.
His face scrunched in the sunlight, thinking.
He turns his legged self on one heel,
he too has that same old posture.

It must be genetic, she said.
Or the boats rolling in off the bay.

Not "bay" he said,
"hay."

2

The invention of memory is a perilous task,
for instance:
I touched her thigh.
Whose thigh, she asks me, scowling.
I hope it isn't *her* thigh
you are touching in the public place of the poem.
It's worse than at a bus stop.
Worse than Peel & Ste. Catherine at noon hour.
Look at all the executives staring at you now,
you idiot.

How much at any given time are
our memories invented.
Or: what is a pure air?

3

The field looks nice with its edging of trees,
trees with real birds,
real nice.
O stop making it so easy on the reader
who wants nice poetry & the line
to stop before the preposition.

Because of the reader's breath (who has been drinking
who knows what anyhow).
Who knows where the reader's mouth has been
seen last
eating ice cream

in Kensington, Calgary, Alberta, Western Canatta.

4

They went to see the rock singer's dress
& plugged their ears during the concert.
Her mouth opened & shut,
they said.
Later in their heads they read her mouth's slippage
& knew what she was singing.

O stop it.
They always knew what she was singing!
Her dress was so many blue flowers!
They had played all her records over & over.
Poplar trees & a field seen up close are both green!

they go to Paris

The caress of wind, nightly,
whooshing over the hay bales.
O get those hay bales outa here,
there's no hay

on the boulevard St. Michel.
Drink a "grand crème" if you can,
if you sit down,
if anyone will take your order.

Je fais restaurant, he said, shrugging her
into the traffic.

O hay, I muttered.

6

it becomes incomprehensible

No hay either in the rue Croix des petits champs,
having dreamed in the dream's silence
of my hand on her thigh
at the crossing of little fields

small twilight
the quiet haybine
a soft hat with its inner hatband worn
next to the skin

all of which is invented
has just been invented now

where there are in fact no fields just
this restaurant voice grating my nerves asking
"vous voulez manger, Madame?"

"justement" j'ai dit

7

We have to invent ourselves continually,
some of us use poems.
"Homes" not "poems" he shouted, that's my
brother, eating more hay
& ruining the line breaks.

What if I went out & did that to his fie-
ld?

8

The perilous task, memory, full
of indeterminate snow.
O hay, she muttered, wanting to get hay
into the absurd fantasy for the nth time,
admitting nothing apart from:

"my hand on her thigh."

Or: her at the metal sink pouring
spring water
into the coffee pot.

Her confidence tremulous under the wire.

Because that's what I thought of!
The way I had to say it
                    "Her confidence tremulous."   So

what
about memory.
What is a pure air?

BIBLIOGRAPHY

Empire, York Street. Toronto: Anansi, 1979. [Out of print.]

The Whiskey Vigil [chapbook]. Madeira Park: Harbour, 1981.

Wanted Alive. Toronto: Anansi, 1983.

Domestic Fuel. Toronto: Anansi, 1985.

Furious. Toronto: Anansi, 1988.

WSW (West South West). Montreal: Véhicule, 1989.

ANTHOLOGIES

Purdy, Al, editor. *Storm Warning 2*. Toronto: McClelland & Stewart, 1976.

Bennett, Donna & Brown, Russell, editors. *An Anthology of Canadian Literature In English. Vol. II*. Toronto: Oxford University Press, 1983.

Norris, Ken, editor. *Canadian Poetry Now, 20 Poets of the '80's*. Toronto: Anansi, 1984.

di Michele, Mary, editor. *Anything Is Possible, A Selection of Eleven Women Poets*. Oakville: Mosaic, 1984.

Landale, Zöe, editor. *Shop Talk*. Vancouver: Pulp Press, 1984.

Lee, Dennis, editor. *The New Canadian Poets 1970-1985*. Toronto: McClelland & Stewart, 1985.

Sullivan, Rosemary, editor. *Poetry by Canadian Women*. Toronto: Oxford, 1989.

Scheier, Libby, Sheard, Sarah, & Wachtel, Eleanor, editors. *Language in Her Eye: Writing and Gender*. Toronto: Coach House Press, 1990.

BRONWEN WALLACE

ONE MORE WOMAN TALKING

Editor's Note: This statement is the edited version of a talk Bronwen Wallace gave as part of a panel on women and language for the feminist caucus of the League of Canadian Poets Annual General Meeting in 1987.

I CAN'T SEPARATE MY PERSONAL POETICS from the life I am leading or from the events that have brought me to this point in it. But since I can't work my whole life history into a statement of poetics, I'll go straight to one of the high points: a day in May, twenty-one years ago, at Queen's University. On that day, I left a provincial meeting of the Student Union for Peace Action with a number of other women (while the men grumbled that we were being "divisive") to meet and discuss what was then being called The Women's Movement. I think I probably left the room because it seemed to be Theoretically Correct to do so. I'd been in the peace movement/new left for about three years at this point; I'd started to read Marx; I was big on being TC. I had absolutely no idea, however, what we would talk about. And I certainly had no idea, theoretically or otherwise, how much this meeting was going to change my life.

What we talked about, in one way or another, for about four hours, were our lives. For me, that meeting represented the first time I had ever been in a room full of women talking *consciously* about their lives, trying to make sense of them, trying to see how the unique and private anecdotes became part of a story that gave each of our lives a public and collective meaning as well.

Since then, the majority of my time has been spent listening to women tell the story of their lives in one form or another. I have attended countless meetings to raise consciousness or disrupt beauty contests or plan anti-nuclear marches; I have listened to women tell about being beaten by husbands or boyfriends; I have held a woman's hand while I gave birth and another's as she lay dying. In being part of these events, I share what is common to many women *and* I also experience them uniquely, as myself. Like every other woman, I come to feminism from my own particular pain and strength and am changed by it as no one else will be ever, while at the same time I participate in events that change us all. The continuing dialectic between these two elements — the public and the private, the unique and the common — is what I enjoy most about living as I do in these particular times.

It is also the basis for my poems. I begin with what I have been given: women's stories, women's conversations. Since most of these stories come to me in pretty straightforward, conversational language, that's what I use in the poem. But as I begin to recreate that conversation on the page, I begin to listen to the voice that tells these stories, a voice that is angry sometimes, or frightened, or grieving or ecstatic. And it becomes the voice I have heard in so many women's conversations, a voice that explores *both* the events in the story itself, *and* something else that lies within those events.

This something else is always a mystery for me, since I never know what the poem will discover (just as I never know, in my day-to-day conversations, what any particular woman will discover). For me that everyday language is a sort of safety net, a familiar place in which a deeper, often more dangerous exploration can take place. These stories, because they are women's stories, have never been heard before. For that reason, content, *what happens*, is extremely important in itself *and also* in what it conveys about a new way of looking at the world, of being in the world. What I hear in "ordinary conversation" is that movement that goes on among us when we feel safe enough or confident enough or loved enough to explore the power within us. This power is so often belittled or denied by the society around us (or by ourselves), but it remains the power by which, in our best moments, we manage to survive and to live, sometimes, with grace. This is what I hear in conversation and what I try to record in my poems. If this sounds like a statement of faith, as much as a statement of poetics, that's because it is.

The questions about language which my writing raises have to do primarily with voice, with how to convey this sense of inner discovery at the heart of the most prosaic anecdote. In that sense, my use of everyday language becomes a challenge for me in the poem, as it is in conversation, when we try to convey matters of life-and-death importance with the same words we also use to order a cheeseburger at Harvey's or teach our children how to swim. Sometimes I think the difference is not as great as we like to think, but mostly I just like the challenge

Another challenge, obviously, lies in the fact that the language I am using has been used in the past primarily to tell men's stories or, more accurately, to tell everyone's stories from a patriarchal point of view. That point of view is embedded in the language itself and one of the questions raised by feminist theory is whether women can speak our piece using it. The following quote from Xavière Gauthier is a typical representation of the issue:

> Women are, in fact, caught in a real contradiction. Throughout the course of history, they have been mute, and it is doubtless by virtue of this mutism that men have been able to speak and write. As long as women remain silent, they will be outside the historical process. But, if they bend to speak and write *as men do*, they will enter history subdued and alienated; it is a history that, logically speaking, their speech should disrupt.

While I definitely experience the problem of the male viewpoint being embedded in language in my own work, I have real difficulty with the way Gauthier (and others who share her view) pose the question and would like to address it in detail. Firstly, I am discouraged — almost offended — by Gauthier's use of "they" rather than "we" in talking about women. It seems to privilege a distant stance that implies theory is somehow separate from our lives.

Also a problem is the notion of women as mute. I just can't see it. I have no trouble seeing Mr. Historian in his study writing his offical Report of the Battle, say, and I have no trouble seeing how the maid brings in his tea and takes it away without a word. In fact, I happen to know that her sister was raped by soldiers after that battle and that her sweetheart was killed in it, I can tell that Mr. H. doesn't even notice her swollen eyes and shaking hands and I'm darn sure none of this will be part of his Account any more than her gossip with the cook will be. BUT I CANNOT, WILL NOT, BELIEVE THAT SHE WAS MUTE ABOUT IT.

Excluded, yes. Mute? Absolutely not!

For one thing, we have other records than those of Mr. H.'s: diaries, journals, letters, recipes, the liturgy of the Craft, lace, home-remedies, quilts, poems, essays and novels, all of which feminist (and other) historians use all the time to develop other histories than the rather limited Patriarchal Record. Why are we judging women by the same standard that has oppressed us?

As to women, by their alleged silence, remaining outside the historical process ... My Great Aunt Nettie, age ninety-four, is telling me a story. In it her father dies when she is three, leaving her mother alone on a farm with several children. That winter, she discovers she has breast cancer. Since she cannot leave the farmwork, she persuades her doctor to come out, chloroform her on the dining room table and remove her breast while her oldest daughter holds the oil-lamp. A few days later, she is back in the barn. She goes on living for another ten years.

This story, out of all her stories, was the one my great aunt chose to give me at the end of her life. I put it in a poem once. I tell you now. So it becomes History.

But — and this is a Great Big But — regardless of what is recorded, the farm exists, the taxes were paid, the kids raised, the crops planted and harvested. My great grandmother can never be *outside* of these. She exists, she persists, she *moves events* as surely as her cells shape my hands, whether they write about her or no. What are we saying about ourselves, about millions of women like her, when we deny her that? Why are we *starting* from a view of history in which women are *always* the victims?

And then there is the issue of talking like a man. On the TV, Margaret Thatcher, a woman who "talks like a man" if I ever heard one. But when I say "talks like a man" I really mean "speaks the language of the Patriarchy" (and by patriarchy I mean a structure originating in households where the father dominated which is reproduced in society in gender relations, language, ways of seeing, etc.). I'm certainly subdued by and alien to such language. I hear it as the language of *power over*, of estrangement, of a system which separates men from women, adults from children, people from other animals, people from nature, in a way that expresses difference as opposition, us versus them, life versus death, etc. It is a history which we must disrupt, I believe, both logically and passionately, because our survival, as a species, depends on it.

I have trouble when the issue is posed in a way which opposes men, *as a gender* to women, *as a gender*, without any reference to the relationship between gender and power, say. It leaves me with the impression that anyone who uses the same syntax, vocabulary, etc. as persons of the male gender are on the side of the devil. Bad guys/good girls. Oppressor/victim. Same old story, just different sides. It's still, as far as I can hear, the patriarchy talking.

Such thinking includes the assumption that "men" and "language" are contained in each other. It's assumed that the patriarchy, that patriarchal language, is a monolith and that women are victimized, determined, totally, by the point of view embedded in it.

Such assumptions, if they remain unquestioned, create a situation in which our discussion of women and language becomes a discussion on men and language because it poses all the questions in the same old way, uses the same old methods of setting things up.

When I write of disrupting or changing history, I begin with the assumption that *people* can change, that we are not totally determined by, *bespoken* by the culture in which we live. I begin, always, with the power of the personal, the private, the unique in each of us, which resists, survives and can change the power that our culture has over us. This is what I have learned from the women's movement and what I try to explore in my poems. I believe that when we speak and write of our lives in this way, we also change language, if only because we say things that have never been said before.

A woman who tells someone that her husband is beating her and she wants it to stop. A man who admits that he is violent and asks for help in changing. A poet who writes a poem that challenges conventional syntax and grammar. A feminist reading of *Jane Eyre*.

A speech by Helen Caldicott. Two women sitting in a bar talking to each other.

For me, all of these change *language*. They change what can be said about women's lives because they disrupt the silence which has covered so much. They change what we think about each other in a culture which accepts things as they are and constantly erodes our power to change even ourselves. They challenge our assumption that how we speak or see or think is neutral, *not* culturally determined. They permit even feminists to have a sense of humour. They embrace passion and anger and even hysteria as appropriate responses to the present danger of the planet.

I personally believe that language will change — and does change — as women's lives change and not because one way of writing or speaking is theoretically correct. I don't think there is one way of writing and speaking that *is* theoretically correct. I'm excited by some of the language theory that forms the basis of Gauthier's statement. Some of it I just can't understand. Some of it simply doesn't correspond with my own experience, either of women or of language. That's generally how I respond to most theories.

What matters to me personally is *being here*, in another room, with another bunch of women, still talking.

❖

BIOGRAPHICAL NOTE

Bronwen Wallace was born in 1945 in Kingston, Ontario, and lived most of her life there. She worked in a transition house for women who were victims of abuse and taught creative writing at Queen's University. Her four collections of poetry and short stories have garnered high praise and many awards — among them the National Magazine Award, the Pat Lowther Award, and the Du Maurier Award for Poetry. In 1989, she was named Regional Winner of the Commonwealth Poetry Prize in the UK With her partner Chris Whynot, she co-directed two doc-umentary films — All You Have To Do, *on learning to live with cancer, and* That's Why I'm Talking, *a celebration of poets and poetry.*

Bronwen Wallace died of cancer in August 1989, in Kingston, at the age of forty-four. Her first collection of short stories, People You'd Trust Your Life To, *published posthumously in 1990, was a national bestseller.*

DAILY NEWS

There are days when I try to imagine the planet
pausing once in a while, like an old woman
on the edge of her bed, who sounds her bones
for the reaches her dying has made
while she slept.

These are the times when I believe
that old men do remember keener weather,
that January when their words froze in the air
or an August so blank with heat
that all it left was the smell
of the crops drying in the fields.
"It's all out of kilter now," one of them tells me,
"just more of the same all year round,"
and I want to believe the planet feels this
as a falling away she wants to tell us about
before it's too late.

Last week, a 20,000-year-old mastodon tusk
was washed up on Virginia Beach.
I believe we should take this
as a direct warning, or better still
a cry for help.

What I want most to believe, though,
is that we're all in this together.

As it is, I hardly know what to look for.
The birthrate's rising slightly, but
according to a recent survey
most teenagers can't see the point
of planning for the future.
Even my friends don't seem to feel
that what they're living these days
is a real life.

Instead, I hear men telling me
that victory is a nuclear war
which 60 million people survive.
I think they really believe this
and what's more, I'm sure it's nothing
to what they can do
whenever they want.

This is the point where I realize
how arrogant it is
to imagine the planet caring about all this.
Though I admit to the image
of a bitter woman longing for a death
that takes her whole family with her,
the mastodon tusk should be enough
to let us know
we're only another species after all.

Meanwhile, my son says he gets scared sometimes
on the way home from school
that they'll drop the bomb
before he makes it.
The worst part though
is how his voice is
when he tells me this.
How he doesn't ask
what he can do about it.

Meanwhile, I read in the papers
that they found a skeleton
that proves whales used to live on land.
And on another page, how doctors managed
to replace a man's left hand with his right
after both were cut off in an accident.
It's going to be okay too, although
"it looks very strange," the man reports.
"Suddenly I'm looking at a hand with fingers.
A hand. It's like getting married
to someone you don't know."

THE MAN WITH THE SINGLE MIRACLE

Here is a man whose life surrounds him
like a house outgrowing its owner.
Surrounds, but doesn't protect. This isn't
safety I'm describing, here
where the morning light gets in
on the sly, prowls around the edges,
sniffing out the dust
before it gathers enough of itself
to pounce. He never gets used to it.
There's always that moment when he can't remember,
when he imagines he's been brought here
drugged, at night, by strangers,
even his hands grown part of some mechanized nightmare,
tools he only operates, but doesn't understand
as they reach for his clothes, the smell and texture
what his body takes for reassurance.

Of course you know the sort of guy I mean,
with a job he likes enough to keep,
a wife he thinks of as his best friend
and kids who seem to be having
the sort of lives he'd hoped they would.
Like all of us, right, this man
whose jaw tightens in the sad part of a movie
though he knows it's really schmaltzy,
who believes they'll find a cure for cancer
before he gets it and assumes that his friends
are much like himself, wary of the way the days grow up
hodgepodge, like those places you find on the backroads
where no one bothers to plan anything.

This is why he is glad when they get together,
drinks and cigarettes, the stories they tell, he loves it
when someone just starts off slowly,
their voice as tentative as a kid's finger
tracing line and squiggle on a page
till DOG or CAT leaps from the paper
in a sudden widening of the eyes.
He loves how his friends build their lives
into stories like that; even he has one
he tries to tell, though it never comes out right.
It's about the witch
who lived at the corner of his street
when he was eight and he always begins with her house
which you couldn't see for all the shrubs and trees
so he tries to explain how it felt, how the air thickened
and the sidewalks narrowed to a breath
you had to squeeze through on your way to the corner store.
At least he wants to make it that slow and heavy,
but his voice always sticks to his heart somehow
and the next thing he knows it's raced right on
to the part where he finds himself
in her kitchen, just staring at her
sitting there in her rocking chair
and how the thing he notices first
is that she is drinking milk
straight from the carton,
sort of pouring it down her throat
the way he does when his mother isn't around,
and he doesn't even know why this is so important,
but it is, so he tries to show them
how it goes with the smell of oilcloth and
onions — that was it — and how that smell fitted

the worn patch of linoleum under her chair,
a patch that warmed to the round, stinging
bite his dime made in his clenched fist.
Except that none of this comes out right
because before he's even finished
his friends start trying to figure out
how he got into the house in the first place;
but once they get going on dreams
or astral projection or some crazy theory
he never has a chance
to tell about being back on the street again
in front of the store, his ice cream
already oozing over his fingers;
or how just as he plunges into it, he raises his eyes
to where the road up ahead ripples and shines,
the whole city gone liquid, rushing
to the tip of his tongue.

You can see his problem, can't you?
And you can see how hard it would be,
getting together with his friends
on Saturdays for drinks and a couple of laughs.
Even the words he'd need, for one thing, belong
in the faces of those creatures
every city tolerates, their ramblings,
if they ever get you to listen,
nearer to prayers than anything else.
Besides, he loves his friends. Even this need
for explanations is something he feels tender about;
how can he help letting them rummage through his story,
the new owners of a place he can't keep up anymore.

This man I'm telling you about
lives in a city near a lake and by January
the harbour's usually frozen over
so that the people who live on the island, two miles out,
start driving to work instead of lining up for the ferry.
Pretty soon there's a good-sized road packed down
where someone in a truck has marked the treacherous spots
with oil drums or old Christmas tress,
though there's hardly a year goes by
that a car doesn't go through.
The city council tries to pass by-laws
forbidding cars on the lake, but by then
everyone's out there, so what can you do.
His kids love it, and every Sunday
they beg to go walking to the island.
Once in a while, he can feel the ice shift under him,
more like sound than motion, how it heaves up
from his feet to his throat, and though he knows
there's no real danger, what he trusts most
is that everyone else is out there too.

Only sometimes, this gets all mixed up, crazy,
like at a party when he'll feel that same
rise and swell pressing into his lungs,
when he looks over at his wife,
laughing in the corner there
or at someone else starting,
a little unsteadily,
towards the kitchen,
and he wants to call to them,
but he can't, any more than he can believe
what he sees; how their deaths
quicken the air around them, stipple their bodies

with a light like the green signals
trees send out before their leaves appear.
All right, he *won't* believe it then,
but doesn't it come to the same thing
for all of us? So frail, how could we bear
this much grace, when it glances
off the odds and ends we've no idea
what to do with, the jumble we just can't
throw out, stuffed into rooms
full of corners, old women
with cartons of milk at their lips
rocking back and forth.

FAMILIARS

That they should come back now,
to this part of my life
and not just through dreams either,
but sidling into daythoughts
with the same unerring timing that they mastered
was it fifteen, no, twenty years ago.
Those two. Zed and Zelda
I called them. For a joke,
though they came to fit their names
or maybe their names, like anyone else's,
came to mean what they were, how
can you tell?
Zed was just that — lean and abrupt,
determined too; I used to imagine her
chain-smoking and giving orders, like Joan Crawford
in *Mildred Pierce*. If there was anything wrong
with the food, Zed let me know, for both of them,
while Zelda sat around grooming herself
all day, always pretty and fluffy, outside
and in, a real airhead; she could have starred
in every beach party movie ever made.
I called her Zelda because I couldn't imagine her
without Zed there, and everyone thought
it was so cute, how she snuggled up to Zed
at night and licked her ears, while Zed kept
one paw around her shoulders, always.
Cute, we all said, how they loved each other
like the kittens on a calendar,
like those cartoon shows

where cats and mice and rabbits
are really humans in disguise
as if the thought of their being anything else
were far too lonely for us to bear.

When Zelda died, Zed found the body.
And after that, she sat in their box
with her face to the wall, howling;
I want to say crying, but that's
wrong too, just as my trying to tell you
how she went skittish and grey, crazy-eyed
like someone on speed, won't explain it either
and anyway, she left about then
so that I only saw her in the alleys
or around the garbage by the pizza place,
though once, a year later, she came back
limping and, well, hardened somehow,
to sit in her old spot for a while
looking out this time, at me
from a distance wider than any
a common language could have filled.

And she's back again. I can feel it,
just as I think I see some of her look
in the one I'm getting
from my own son these days, the one
he brings out during the argument
we're always having, the argument
neither of us can ever win
(and which winning wouldn't matter anyway)
the one that began with his first word
and slowly clarifies itself, like a photograph
in a developing tray, what my son holds up

as evidence: the life he sees
out there, away, in the future.
At 13, he carries
the little I've had time to give him
easily, just as I hope he'll lose,
someday, the weight of my failings
which are heavy now, like the scorn
he bears me. *I love you* I say to him
I love you, almost afraid,
like when I was a kid and believed
you could only use a word so many times
before it flickered out, a flashlight
with a dead battery.

So, lots of times I talk to him
inside my head, though I don't like to.
It's too much like the conversations
I catch myself having
with a friend who's died, when I want to say
you and mean it, unable to believe
I can't anymore, just as I can't imagine
her body, sunk through death
until the earth's become the only air
it takes in and releases, more slowly,
more surely, year after year.
This is the power she'll have for me
always. As my son will.
It's why the cats are back. Those two,
Zed and Zelda, and then just Zed,
that crazy grey cat out there, past
the reach of our comfort, our human

laughter, that other animal
come back, in broad day, to sit
in this room with me and stare
from across it all

FOOD

for Marty, and in memory of Jessie Glaberman

Begin where we all do
with milk. How I still like mine
straight from the cow, driving out
to a farm each week, through fields
dotted with Holsteins, the only landscape
I can understand. My dad says the stuff
that's really worth drinking's
squirted warm and straight from the teat
and I believe him, just as I know
his city life's the instrument
that pries that memory loose
from the history he hated, the narrow
caked path from pasture to barn
and the blistered sun at his neck
day after day. Just as I know
for me, too, it's more nostalgia
in the glass, as even the smallest farms
become factories, the cows hooked up
from udder to tank to truck
to pasteurization plant
and on (in just a few years, probably)
to what's become of beef or chicken, things
kept in buildings never opened to the sun.

Food. Or the politics of food. You see
I did learn what you tried to teach me, you two:
your house on Bewick Avenue, your table
where a union man from Bologna might meet up
with a woman from a feminist commune

in New Mexico or a kid from Oregon, on the road
for the summer, who'd heard about your place,
everybody hashing out their differences
over meals that went on for as long
as our appetites lasted and the wine held,
Jessie at her end, pushing her glasses up
with one hand, passing food with the other,
Marty at his, finger out, making some
theoretical point someone else had overlooked,
living up to the joke we made of his habit,
as soon as he'd open his mouth, we'd laugh
and call out "and then Lenin said ... "
loving him for it.

Just as I love you, Marty,
for that whole hot summer
when you taught me to read *Capital*
of all things, as I thought no book
could be read, cold theory warmed
by those hands of yours, the lines
that oil and grit had eaten there
part of what you were saying, just as the smell
that clings to hair and clothes gives off
the heat of a factory, the noise,
fights with foremen, meetings, wildcats,
always at it, "The working class
is revolutionary or it is nothing" — Karl Marx.
"But not a slogan," I can hear you saying,
"a statement of fact; either we'll manage
to change things or we'll disappear,"
your finger out as you say this, the other hand
reaching for chicken or coffee, refusing
to separate food from what it costs.

Jessie, in the only snapshot I have
your mouth's open, of course, your face
blurred by what you were saying at the moment,
words freed as carelessly as the smoke
from your cigarettes, filling the air
and disappearing. At your end of the table
everything was always up for grabs;
"Spit it out," you'd cry, when we fumbled
for a straighter phrase, "don't be afraid
to say what isn't finished, what seems
crazy. Just say what you can;
we'll look at it together."
And we would. All of us,
peering into those dimmer, tangled
regions theory doesn't open on
and though I bet we'd argue still
about what got said those nights,
we'd all be hearing your voice
angry, laughing, leading us into them.
Oh, Jessie, it drives me crazy
knowing you died alone,
how you must have hated, struggled
and in another movement,
taken it, knowing we are always
alone in this, your shrug
— I can see it still — what I have
of you, your work
that widening of the wild zone
between the power to fight what happens to us
and the power to accept what is.

It's late afternoon in the old house on Bewick.

In the kitchen, someone's poking around
trying to decide what to have for dinner,
while in his new apartment
Marty follows an argument about Poland
from the stove, where he's making
his famous stir-fry, a recipe
I'll use myself tonight, with tomatoes
and zucchini from my garden, snow peas
from the guy in the third stall, second row
at the market, soy and ginger, Basmati rice
from I don't know where, and while we eat
I'll tell my family how I heard
on the radio today the future's
in kiwi fruit, a new type, hairless
and the size of grapefruit, more vitamin C
than a dozen oranges and easier to ship.
I'll tell them how scientists
have developed an apple tree
shaped like a telephone pole, no branches,
fruit straight from the stem, for easier
picking and bigger profits and while we
take this in, women I've eaten with
are adding sour cream and red wine
to their pot roasts, as Jessie
taught them to. For all I know,
they're quoting Lenin and Marx,
maybe the FBI is right, subversion
is everywhere.
Oh, I know, I know, it's late
in the century, the revolution hasn't come,
the hungry go on, food costs the earth,
the work of getting enough
breaks us all, I know, I know,

but even so, the tomatoes
are red, ready to sting
my tongue, the smell of their vines
clings to my arms, Marty talks
with his mouth full, his finger
urgent as always, a woman throws
a handful of parsley in the pot, a taste
brings me up to her, and it's that
I'm telling for the moment, just
for now.

ANNIVERSARY

in memoriam, Pat Logan

The road turns off
just where it always does and rising
comes out to the second corner
where the graveyard is.
Your grave. You. Behind us,
in one of those reforestation stands
the government plants, the pines
grow taller in their narrow columns
as if to show me how there can be order
in returning what we owe.
I remember what someone told me
of a woman whose husband took her ashes,
as she'd asked him to, and with their children
traveled for a year to scatter them
all over the world, a gesture
that tries to say what death allows
in each of us, no matter how we meet it.

It makes me want
to tell you everything:
what I ate for breakfast,
my son's French teacher's name,
how my basil's doing this year
or the deal I got on this Lincoln rocker
from an antique place I've just discovered
on the Wilmer Road. The man there — you'd like
him, Pat — who told me how he'd farmed
for years and years and then risked everything
on something else he loved,

his hands stroking a desk or chair
just as they've bumped the right curve
of a cow's belly, learning the season
of the calf within, listening to wood now,
what to bring forth
from layers of decisions made by strangers,
for their own good reasons.

Remember that day you taught me
how to look for four-leaf clovers?
"Don't try so hard," you kept saying,
"just peek from the corner of your eye,
like this," running your fingers
through a patch and coming up with one
every time, surprised as I was
and with no more faith, but opening
your hand out anyway, that gesture
which belongs to any gamble,
no matter how crazy, the movement
by which a life gets changed
for keeps, a reach
for what we only hope
is there

just as this yearly journey reaches
deeper into what I only thought
I understood: your death
is final, and touching that
brings out the colours — certain
as the grain in oak or cherry —
of a wider life that grows
through the small demands the present makes
pushing me back to the car for the ride home,

already planning the sandwich I'll get
at the truck stop on the highway; empty now,
the woman who runs it taking the time
to put her feet up, sink back
into the knowledge that will hold her
until I arrive; my wave, her smile
what we'll begin with, the common
courtesies, as if they were nothing
to be surprised by.

KOKO

"Hands developed with terrible labor by apes
Hang from the sleeves of evangelists ..."
                    — Robert Bly in
                  "The Great Society"

Only now it is our terrible labour
(or what we thought was ours, alone)
unfurling from the root-black fingers
of an ape. Koko, the talking gorilla.
In Ameslan, her hands are muscular
and vibrant as vocal cords, name
colours and distinguish *bad* and *will*,
can make a metaphor; they choose
a tailless kitten for a pet
and christen him *All-Ball*, lie
when they need to and insult their trainer
Penny dirty toilet devil, a repertoire
of over 500 words that upset
Descartes, Marx, our known,
human world. Not to mention fellow linguists
who say it's all a trick — Polly, Polly
pretty bird or Mr. Ed. They point
to her IQ score, a meagre 85,
though when they asked if she'd choose
a tree or a house for shelter
from the rain, she chose a tree
and got marked wrong.

Who says
and what
is what it comes to, though,
the sky filling up with satellites,
the cities with paper, whole stores
of greeting cards for everything
we can't spit out ourselves,
like the scratch at the back of the brain
we no longer recognize as memory.

On the TV Reagan and Gorbachev in Geneva,
though their names don't matter much,
just two more faces over shirts and ties
discussing missile size, the "nitty-gritty"
as a spokesman puts it, while
"women are more interested in peace
and things of that nature ...
the human interest stuff."

The human interest.
Kinda like the swings in the park
across from here, how they always
squeak, day in, day out.
The guys who trim the grass
and keep the benches painted
don't even try to fix them anymore;
they know some things are like that,
stubborn as hell, no matter how much
you make an hour or what kind of government
you get. So that what we have are humans
in Oslo, Leningrad, Peking, Thunder Bay,
Denver, Cordoba and Rome pushing their kids

on swings that *squeak   squeak   squeak*
like the creaks
and farts and stutterings the body makes
to say *here and here and here.*

After living with them,
Jane Goodall found that chimpanzees
use tools, which leaves us language
as the last thing
we've got, we think,
and at the compound, Koko looking out,
a reporter tries to keep it:

"Are you an animal or a person?"

The hands coming up, almost
before he's done: *Fine animal gorilla.*
Close to the chest, showing him
familiar palm and fingers
sing *fine* caress *animal.*

BIBLIOGRAPHY

With Mary di Michele. *Bread and Chocolate/ Marrying into the Family*. Ottawa: Oberon, 1980.

Signs of the Former Tenant. Ottawa: Oberon, 1983.

Common Magic. Ottawa: Oberon, 1985.

The Stubborn Particulars of Grace. Toronto: McClelland & Stewart, 1987.

People You'd Trust Your Life To. Toronto: McClelland & Stewart, 1990.

Keep That Candle Burning Bright and Other Poems. Toronto: Coach House Press, 1991.

The Selected Journalism of Bronwen Wallace. Kingston: Quarry Press, forthcoming 1992.

ANTHOLOGIES (SELECTED)

Wayman, Tom, editor. *Going for Coffee*. Vancouver: Harbour Publishing, 1980.

LaDuke, Janice & Luxton, Steve, editors. *Full Moon*. Dunvegan: Quadrant Editions, 1983.

di Michele, Mary, editor. *Anything Is Possible, A Selection of Eleven Women Poets*. Oakville: Mosaic, 1984.

Lee, Dennis, editor. *The New Canadian Poets 1970-1985*. Toronto: McClelland & Stewart, 1985.

Geddes, Gary, editor. *Fifteen Canadian Poets x2*. Toronto: Oxford, 1988.

The Journey Anthology. Toronto: McClelland and Stewart, 1989.

Nemiroff, Greta, editor. *Celebrating Women: Poetry and Short Stories by and about Canadian Women*. Toronto: Fitzhenry and Whiteside, 1989.

Sullivan, Rosemary, editor. *Poetry by Canadian Women*. Toronto: Oxford, 1989.

RHEA TREGEBOV is the editor of *Frictions: Stories by Women*. She is the author of three books of poetry. Born in Saskatoon and raised in Winnipeg, she has lived in Toronto since 1978.

OTHER BOOKS FROM SECOND STORY PRESS:

Aunt Fred Is A Witch *Gilmore*

The Amazing Adventure of LittleFish *Hébert*

As For the Sky, Falling:
A Critical Look at Psychiatry and Suffering *Supeene*

Beyond Hope *Zaremba*

Canadian Feminism and the Law.
The Women's Legal Education and Action Fund and the
Pursuit of Equality *Razack*

The Extraordinary Ordinary Everything Room *Tregebov*

Ezzie's Emerald *McDonnell*

Frictions: Stories by Women *Tregebov*

Franny and the Music Girl *Hearn*

In the Name of the Fathers:
The Story Behind Child Custody *Crean*

Infertility: Old Myths, New Meanings *Rehner*

A Monster in My Cereal *Hébert*

Menopause: A Well Woman Book *Montreal Health Press*

Of Customs and Excise: Short Fiction *Mara*

Pornography and the Sex Crisis *Cole*

A Reason to Kill *Zaremba*

The Summer Kid *Levy*

Uneasy Lies *Zaremba*

WhenIwasalittlegirl *Gilmore*

Work for a Million *Zaremba*

The Y Chromosome *Gom*